Pocket SAN FRANCISCO

TOP SIGHTS • LOCAL LIFE • MADE EASY

Mariella Krause, Alison Bing, John A Vlahides

In This Book

QuickStart Guide

Your keys to understanding the city – we help you decide what to do and how to do it

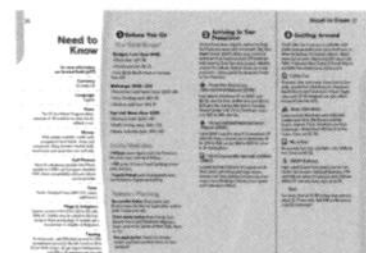

Need to Know
Tips for a smooth trip

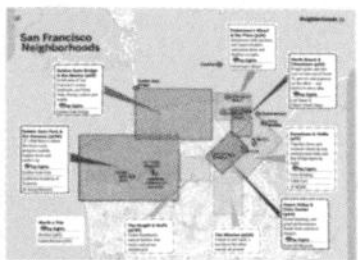

Neighborhoods
What's where

Explore San Francisco

The best things to see and do, neighborhood by neighborhood

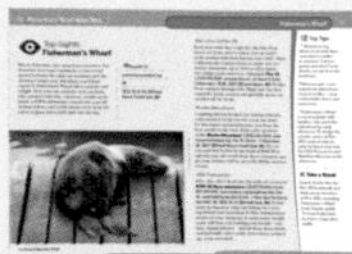

Top Sights
Make the most of your visit

Local Life
The insider's city

The Best of San Francisco

The city's highlights in handy lists to help you plan

Best Walks
See the city on foot

San Francisco's Best...
The best experiences

Survival Guide

Tips and tricks for a seamless, hassle-free city experience

Getting Around
Travel like a local

Essential Information
Including where to stay

Our selection of the city's best places to eat, drink and experience:

Sights

Eating

Drinking

Entertainment

Shopping

These symbols give you the vital information for each listing:

- Telephone Numbers
- Opening Hours
- Parking
- Nonsmoking
- Internet Access
- Wi-Fi Access
- Vegetarian Selection
- English-Language Menu
- Family-Friendly
- Pet-Friendly
- Bus
- Ferry
- Metro
- Subway
- Tram
- Train

Find each listing quickly on maps for each neighborhood:

Lonely Planet's San Francisco

Lonely Planet Pocket Guides are designed to get you straight to the heart of the city.

Inside you'll find all the must-see sights, plus tips to make your visit to each one really memorable. We've split the city into easy-to-navigate neighborhoods and provided clear maps so you'll find your way around with ease. Our expert authors have searched out the best of the city: walks, food, nightlife and shopping, to name a few. Because you want to explore, our 'Local Life' pages will take you to some of the most exciting areas to experience the real San Francisco.

And of course you'll find all the practical tips you need for a smooth trip: itineraries for short visits, how to get around, and how much to tip the guy who serves you a drink at the end of a long day's exploration.

It's your guarantee of a really great experience.

Our Promise

You can trust our travel information because Lonely Planet authors visit the places we write about, each and every edition. We never accept freebies for positive coverage, so you can rely on us to tell it like it is.

QuickStart Guide 7

Explore San Francisco 21

Worth a Trip:

The Best of San Francisco 157

San Francisco's Best Walks

San Francisco's Best...

Survival Guide 177

BGRISSOM/SHUTTERSTOCK ©

QuickStart Guide

Welcome to San Francisco

Grab your coat and a handful of glitter, and enter the land of fog and fabulousness. If there's a skateboard move yet to be busted, a technology still unimagined, a green scheme untested or quirk left uncelebrated, chances are it's about to happen here. So long, inhibitions; hello, San Francisco.

Downtown vista from Alamo Square Park (p134)
CANADASTOCK/SHUTTERSTOCK ©

San Francisco Top Sights

ALESSANDRO COLLE/SHUTTERSTOCK ©

Golden Gate Bridge (p24)

An iconic art-deco masterpiece.

Alcatraz (p48)

Notorious former prison on an island.

MINTIMAGES/SHUTTERSTOCK ©

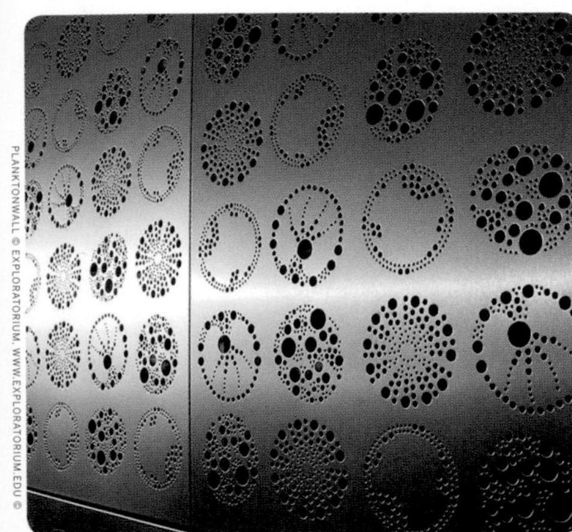

Exploratorium (p50)

Hands-on science fun for all ages.

Golden Gate Park (p142)

A thousand-acre urban playground.

Ferry Building (p74)

Foodie nirvana in a historic building.

JOSHUA RAINEY PHOTOGRAPHY/SHUTTERSTOCK ©

LYNN Y/SHUTTERSTOCK ©

de Young Museum (p146)

Even the building is a work of art.

San Francisco Museum of Modern Art (p80)

Always fabulous and newly expanded.

MITCHELL FUNK/GETTY IMAGES ©

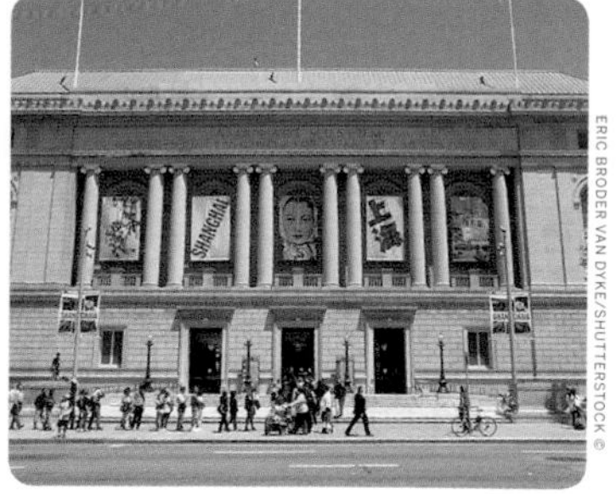

ERIC BRODER VAN DYKE/SHUTTERSTOCK ©

Asian Art Museum (p96)

The largest collection outside of Asia.

Cable Cars (p76)

The ultimate urban carnival ride.

WONWOO LEE/GETTY IMAGES ©

California Academy of Sciences (p144)

Forty thousand creatures to greet you.

ANTON_IVANOV/SHUTTERSTOCK ©

STEFFEN LAY/SHUTTERSTOCK ©

Fisherman's Wharf (p36)

Don't miss the sea lions.

ZRFPHOTO/GETTY IMAGES ©

Coit Tower & Filbert Steps (p54)

Panoramas, wild parrots and a workout.

San Francisco Local Life

Local experiences and hidden gems to help you uncover the real city

The city with its head perpetually in the clouds is also surprisingly down to earth. Dive into San Francisco's neighborhoods to observe its outlandish ideas in action, from graffiti-art-gallery alleyways to certified green saloons.

The History-Making Castro (p128)

☑Gay-history landmarks ☑LGBT community organizations

DIEGO GRANDI/SHUTTERSTOCK ©

Sunny Mission Stroll (p112)

☑ Slacker hotspots ☑ Mural-lined alleyways

Dear Face, by artist Emily Glaubinger

KOBBY DAGAN/SHUTTERSTOCK ©

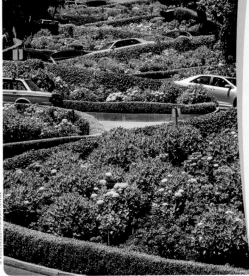

TRAVELVIEW/SHUTTERSTOCK ©

Russian Hill & Nob Hill Secrets (p70)

☑ Stairway walks ☑ Inspiration points

Other great places to experience the city like a local:

- Off the Grid at Fort Mason (p30)
- Downtown Roof Gardens (p92)
- Hush-Hush Hooch (p106)
- Giants Game Seats (p90)
- Coasting the Coast (p152)
- Heart of the City Farmers Market (p103)
- Cooking in the Mission (p119)
- Twitter's Controversial HQ (p102)
- Skate the Haight (p135)

San Francisco Day Planner

Day One

Leap onto the Powell-Mason cable car for hills and thrills. Hop off in North Beach and hike to **Coit Tower** (p54) for groundbreaking murals and giddy, 360-degree panoramas. Take scenic **Filbert Street Steps** to the sunny Embarcadero waterfront, then plunge into the total darkness of the Tactile Dome inside the **Exploratorium** (p50).

Catch your prebooked ferry to **Alcatraz** (p49), where D-Block solitary raises goosebumps. Make your escape, taking in **Golden Gate Bridge** (p24) views on the ferry ride back. Take the Powell-Mason cable car to North Beach to take in free-speech landmark **City Lights** (p58) and mingle with SF's freest spirits at the **Beat Museum** (p59).

Since you just escaped prison, you're tough enough to handle too-close-for-comfort comics at **Cobb's Comedy Club** (p67) or razor-sharp satire at **Beach Blanket Babylon** (p66). Toast the wildest night in the west with potent Pisco sours at **Comstock Saloon** (p64) or spiked cappuccinos at **Tosca Cafe** (p62).

Day Two

Hop the N Judah to **Golden Gate Park** (p142) to see carnivorous plants enjoying insect breakfasts at the **Conservatory of Flowers** (p143). Follow Andy Goldsworthy's artful sidewalk fault line into the **de Young Museum** (p146), then take a walk on the wild side in the rainforest dome of the **California Academy of Sciences** (p144). Enjoy a moment of Zen with green tea at the **Japanese Tea Garden** (p143) and bliss out in the secret redwood grove at the **San Francisco Botanical Garden** (p143).

Join surfers at **Outerlands** (p150) for artisan grilled cheese and organic soup, then beachcomb **Ocean Beach** (p150) to the **Beach Chalet** (p153) to glimpse 1930s Works Progress Administration (WPA) murals celebrating San Francisco. Follow the **Coastal Trail** (p152) past Sutro Baths and Land's End, and watch fog tumble over **Golden Gate Bridge** (p24) and Impressionist dancers twirl at the **Legion of Honor** (p150).

Watch the sun go down over the Pacific, then gear up for live music at the **Independent** (p137) or **Hotel Utah** (p91), or a drag show at **Aunt Charlie's Lounge** (p105) or **Oasis** (p90).

Short on time?
We've arranged San Francisco's must-sees into these day-by-day itineraries to make sure you see the very best of the city in the time you have available.

Day Three

Take the California St cable car to pagoda-topped Grant St for an eye-opening **Red Blossom Tea Company** (p65) tea tasting and then a jaw-dropping history of Chinatown at the **Chinese Historical Society of America** (p58). Wander temple-lined Waverly Pl and notorious Ross Alley to find your fortune at the **Golden Gate Fortune Cookie Company** (p68).

Hail dim sum carts for dumplings at **City View** (p64), then head uphill past Commercial St's former Gold rush 'parlor houses' (read: brothels) to catch the Powell-Hyde cable car. Past zigzagging **Lombard Street** (p41) you'll reach **Maritime Museum** (p41), where 1930s mosaics reveal underwater worlds. Save the planet from Space Invaders at **Musée Mécanique** (p37), or enter underwater stealth mode inside a real WWII submarine: **USS Pampanito** (p37).

Browse Hayes Valley boutiques before your concert at the **San Francisco Symphony** (p107) or **SFJAZZ Center** (p106); and toast your good fortune at **Smuggler's Cove** (p105).

Day Four

Wander 24th St past mural-covered bodegas to **Balmy Alley** (p116), where the Mission muralist movement began in the 1970s. Stop for a 'secret breakfast' (bourbon and cornflakes) ice-cream sundae at **Humphry Slocombe** (p119). Pause for pirate supplies at **826 Valencia** (p116) and duck into **Clarion Alley** (p112), an outdoor graffiti-art gallery. See San Francisco's first building, Spanish adobe **Mission Dolores** (p117), and visit the memorial to the Ohlone laborer who built it.

Spot Victorian 'Painted Ladies' on your way to hilltop **Alamo Square Park** (p134) for downtown vistas. Stroll tree-lined Panhandle park, then window-shop your way down hippie-historic Haight St past record stores, vintage emporiums, and drag designers.

Place orders at **Rosamunde Sausage Grill** (p135) to enjoy with your pick of 400 microbrews at **Toronado** (p136). Don't miss showtime at deco-fabulous **Castro Theatre** (p129), where shows begin with a crowd sing-along.

Need to Know

For more information, see Survival Guide (p177)

Currency
US dollar ($)

Language
English

Visas
The US Visa Waiver Program allows nationals of 38 countries to enter the US without a visa.

Money
ATMs widely available; credit cards accepted at most hotels, stores and restaurants. Many farmers-market stalls, food trucks and some bars are cash only.

Cell Phones
Most US cell phones besides the iPhone operate on CDMA, not European-standard GSM; check compatibility with your phone service provider.

Time
Pacific Standard Time (GMT/UTC minus eight hours)

Plugs & Adapters
Electric current in the USA is 110 to 115 volts, 60Hz AC. Outlets may be suited for flat two-prong or three-prong plugs. If needed, get a transformer or adapter at Walgreens.

Tipping
At restaurants, add 15% (bad service) to 25% (exceptional service) to the bill. Count on $1 to $2 per drink at bars, $2 per bag to hotel porters, and 15% or $1 minimum per taxi ride.

1 Before You Go

Your Daily Budget

Budget: Less than $150

- Dorm bed: $33–60
- Food-truck fare: $5–13
- Live North Beach music or comedy: free–$15

Midrange: $150–350

- Downtown hotel/home-share: $130–180
- Ferry Building meal: $18–45
- Alcatraz night tour: $44.25

Top end: More than $350

- Boutique hotel: $180–380
- Chef's tasting menu: $60–228
- Opera orchestra seats: $90–140

Useful Websites

- **SFGate** (www.sfgate.com) *San Francisco Chronicle* news and event listings.
- **7x7** (www.7x7.com) Trend-spotting restaurants and bars.
- **Lonely Planet** (www.lonelyplanet.com/san-francisco) Expert local advice.

Advance Planning

Two months before Book hotels and Alcatraz tours for May to September; walk to build stamina for hills.

Three weeks before Book Precita Eyes Mission mural and Chinatown Alleyways tours; reserve for dinner at Rich Table, Benu or Coi.

One week before Search for theater tickets and find out what else is on next weekend.

2 Arriving in San Francisco

Service from three airports makes reaching San Francisco quick and convenient. Big Area Rapid Transit (BART) offers easy access to downtown San Francisco from SFO and Oakland airports; from San Jose airport, shuttles connect to Caltrain. Amtrak trains are a low-emissions, scenic option for domestic travel to San Francisco.

From San Francisco International Airport (SFO)

Fast rides to downtown SF on BART cost $8.95; door-to-door shuttle vans cost $17 to $20, plus tip; express bus fare to Transbay Transit Center is $2.25 via SamTrans; taxis cost $40 to $55, plus tip.

From Oakland International Airport (OAK)

Catch BART from the airport to downtown SF ($10.20); take a shared van to downtown SF for $30 to $40; or pay $60 to $80 for a taxi to SF destinations.

From Emeryville Amtrak station (EMY)

Located outside Oakland, this depot serves West Coast and nationwide train routes; Amtrak runs free shuttles to/from San Francisco's Ferry Building, Caltrain, Civic Center and Fisherman's Wharf.

3 Getting Around

Small, hilly San Francisco is walkable, with public transportation and occasional taxis or bikes for backup. For transit options, departures and arrivals, check www.511.org or call ☎511. A detailed Muni Street & Transit Map is available free online (www.sfmta.com).

Cable Car

Frequent, slow and scenic, from 6am to 1am daily; joyride from downtown to Chinatown, North Beach and Fisherman's Wharf. Single rides cost $7; for frequent use, get a Muni Passport (per day $21).

M Muni Streetcar

Lines connect downtown and SoMa with Golden Gate Park, the Mission and the Castro. Historic F-line streetcars run from Fisherman's Wharf down Market St to the Castro. Fares are $2.50.

Muni Bus

Reasonably fast, but schedules vary wildly by line. Fares are $2.50.

S BART Subway

High-speed transit from downtown to Civic Center, the Mission, Oakland/Berkeley, SFO and Millbrae, where it connects with Caltrain. Within SF, one-way fares start at $1.95.

Taxi

Taxi fares start at $3.50 at flag drop and run about $2.75 per mile. Add 15% to the fare as a tip ($1 minimum).

San Francisco Neighborhoods

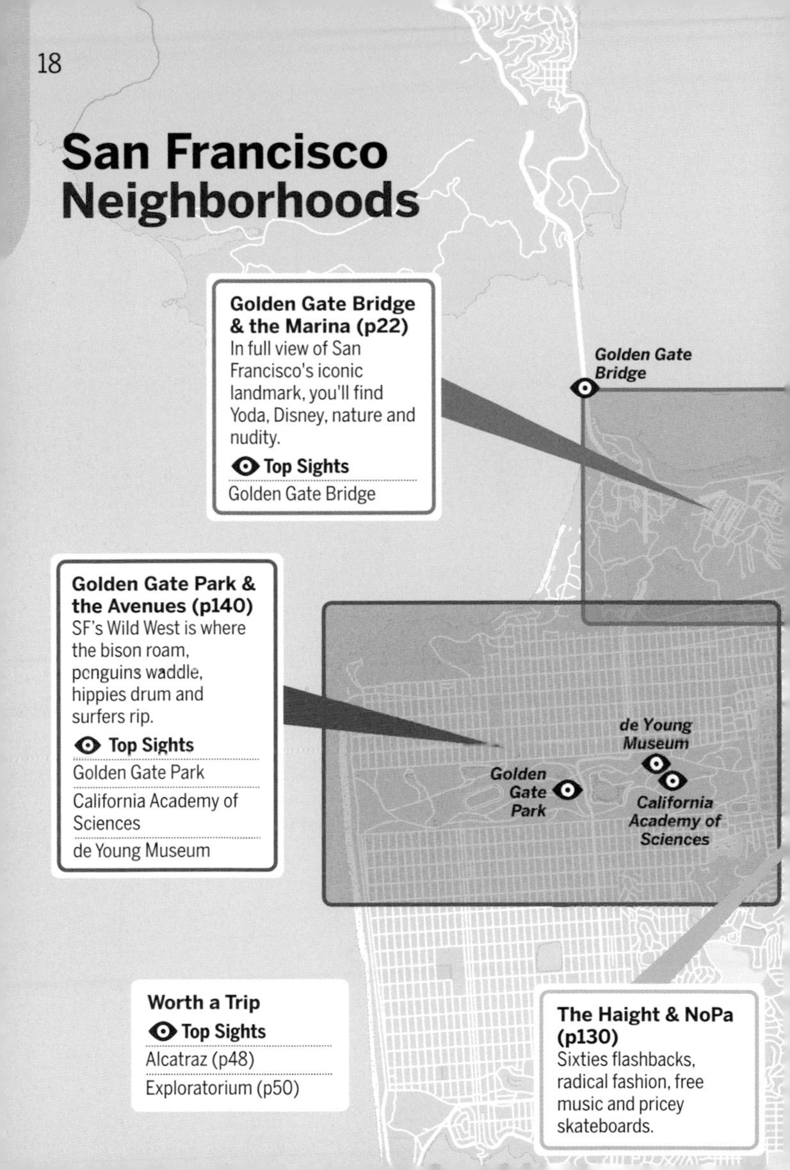

Golden Gate Bridge & the Marina (p22)
In full view of San Francisco's iconic landmark, you'll find Yoda, Disney, nature and nudity.

Top Sights

Golden Gate Bridge

Golden Gate Park & the Avenues (p140)
SF's Wild West is where the bison roam, penguins waddle, hippies drum and surfers rip.

Top Sights

Golden Gate Park

California Academy of Sciences

de Young Museum

Worth a Trip

Top Sights

Alcatraz (p48)

Exploratorium (p50)

The Haight & NoPa (p130)
Sixties flashbacks, radical fashion, free music and pricey skateboards.

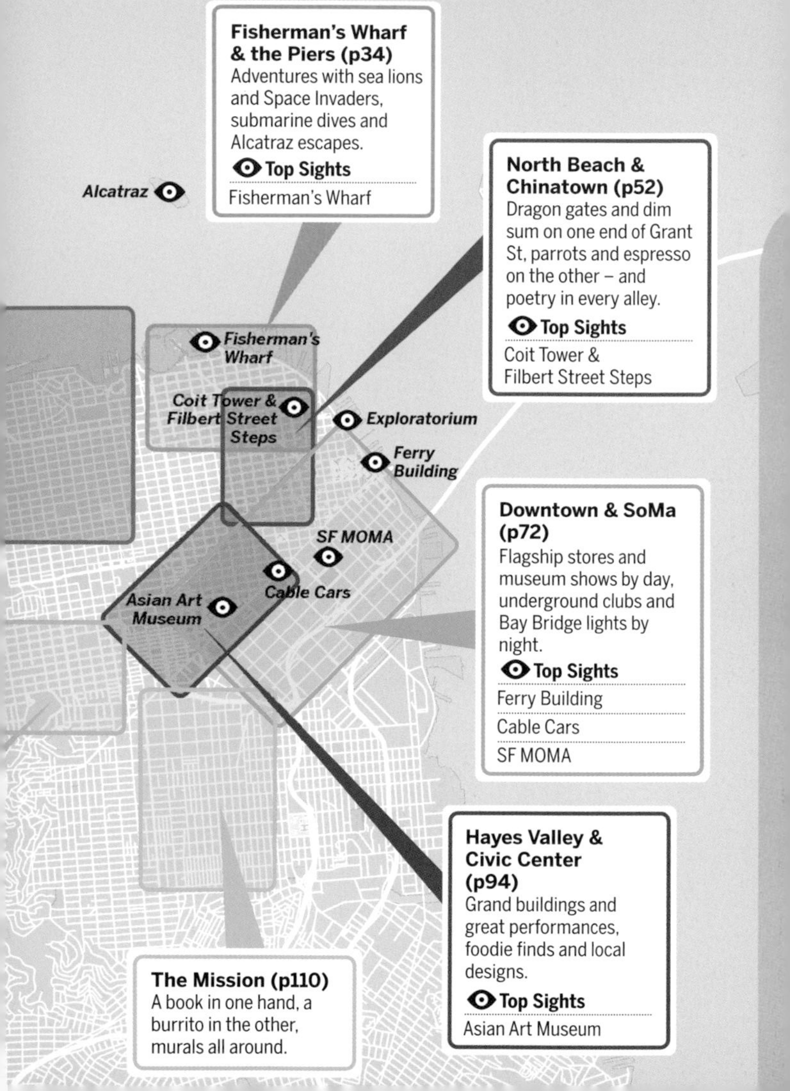

Fisherman's Wharf & the Piers (p34)
Adventures with sea lions and Space Invaders, submarine dives and Alcatraz escapes.

Top Sights

Fisherman's Wharf

North Beach & Chinatown (p52)
Dragon gates and dim sum on one end of Grant St, parrots and espresso on the other – and poetry in every alley.

Top Sights

Coit Tower & Filbert Street Steps

Downtown & SoMa (p72)
Flagship stores and museum shows by day, underground clubs and Bay Bridge lights by night.

Top Sights

Ferry Building

Cable Cars

SF MOMA

Hayes Valley & Civic Center (p94)
Grand buildings and great performances, foodie finds and local designs.

Top Sights

Asian Art Museum

The Mission (p110)
A book in one hand, a burrito in the other, murals all around.

Explore San Francisco

Worth a Trip

Golden Gate Bridge (p24)

Explore

Golden Gate Bridge & the Marina

The waterfront neighborhood near Golden Gate Bridge has chic boutiques, outrageous theater, and food trucks in a former army depot – but 120 years ago it reeked of dirty laundry and drunken cows (swanky Union St was once Cow Hollow, where clothes were cleaned and cows munched mash from whiskey stills). Today's spiffy Marina was mostly built in the 1930s atop 1906 earthquake debris.

The Sights in a Day

Browse boutiques for local designs and stylish bargains on Union and Chestnut Sts. Head to **Fort Mason Center** (p28) for organic **Greens** (p30) chili takeout by the bay-front docks, then coffee at the **Interval Bar & Cafe** (p31) under Brian Eno's trippy digital paintings.

Wander the Marina waterfront, from the **Wave Organ** (p29) past the picturesque **Palace of Fine Arts** (p28) and into **Crissy Field** (p28) for sweeping Golden Gate Bridge views. Pop into the **Warming Hut** (p30) for nature-book browsing, or hike onward to Civil War–era **Fort Point** (p25) for a Hitchcock-worthy view of the bridge's ribbed orange underbelly. If you've got another couple of miles in you before sunset, walk across the **Golden Gate Bridge** (p24).

Take the bus back toward Union St to hit happy hour at **West Coast Wine & Cheese** (p31) before your reservations at **A16** (p29). Enjoy a play at **Magic Theatre** (p32), or an improv performance at **BATS** (p32).

Top Sights

Golden Gate Bridge (p24)

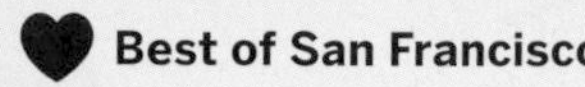

Best of San Francisco

Outdoors

Crissy Field (p28)

Baker Beach (p28)

Architecture

Golden Gate Bridge (p24)

Palace of Fine Arts (p28)

Eating Out

Off the Grid (p30)

Getting There

Bus Buses 47 and 49 connect the Marina to downtown; 41, 30 and 45 run to North Beach; 43 connects to the Haight; 22 runs to the Mission.

Car There's parking at Fort Mason and Crissy Field, and free parking in the adjoining Presidio.

Top Sights
Golden Gate Bridge

The city's most spectacular icon towers 80 stories above the roiling waters of the Golden Gate, the narrow entrance to San Francisco Bay. When afternoon fog rolls in, poof! The Golden Gate Bridge disappears. Most mornings it reappears, orange against blue skies – a trick assisted by 25 daredevil painters, who apply 1000 gallons of 'International Orange' each week.

Map p26, A1

toll information 877-229-8655

www.goldengatebridge.org/visitors

Hwy 101

northbound free, southbound $6.50-7.50

28, all Golden Gate Transit buses

Golden Gate Bridge

Vista Points

San Franciscans have passionate perspectives on every subject, but especially their signature landmark. Fog aficionados prefer the north-end lookout at Marin's Vista Point to watch clouds tumble over bridge cables. Crissy Field is a key spot to appreciate the span in its entirety, with windsurfers and kite-fliers adding action to your snapshots. From clothing-optional Baker Beach, you can see the bridge's backside in all its naked glory.

Fort Point

Completed in 1861 with 126 cannons, **Fort Point** (☎415-556-1693; www.nps.gov/fopo; Marine Dr; admission free; ⏰10am-5pm Fri-Sun; P; 🚌28) stood guard against certain invasion by Confederate soldiers during the Civil War...or not. This heavily armed fort saw no action – at least until Alfred Hitchcock shot scenes from *Vertigo* here, with stunning views of the Golden Gate Bridge from below. Enter the fortress to checkout 19th-century historical displays – including surprisingly tasty military menus – and climb to rooftop viewing decks for close-up glimpses of the bridge's underbelly, and hear the whoosh of traffic overhead.

Bridge Crossings

To see both sides of the Golden Gate, hike or bike the span. From the parking area and bus stop, a pedestrian pathway leads past the toll plaza to the east sidewalk (pedestrian access 5am to 6:30pm daily). Near the toll plaza is a cross section of suspension cable, with the tensile strength to support thousands of cars and buses daily. If you'd rather not walk back, Golden Gate Transit buses head back to SF from Marin. Bikes have 24-hour bridge access via either sidewalk, but must yield to pedestrians on the east sidewalk. Electric bikes must be powered down during bridge crossings.

☑ Top Tips

- Carpools (three or more) are free 5am to 9am and 4pm to 6pm.
- Dress warmly before crossing the bridge on foot or bike, with a water-resistant outer layer to break the wind and fog.
- Skating and pets (except guide animals) are not allowed on bridge sidewalks. Wheelchairs are permitted on the east sidewalk.
- Glimpse the underbelly of the bridge from the Municipal Pier in front of the Warming Hut. Fort Point staff demonstrate how to catch crabs here (by reservation Saturday mornings March to October).

✕ Take a Break

Stop by the certified green Warming Hut (p30) for fair-trade coffee and pastries.

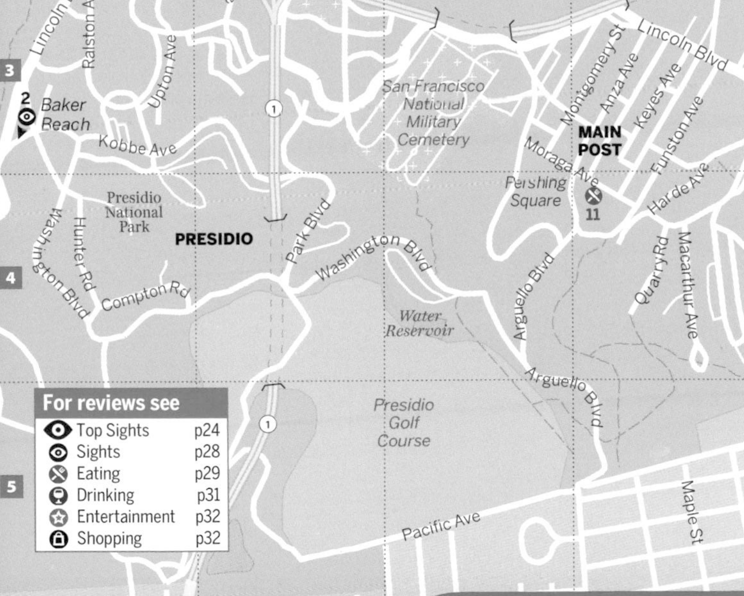

For reviews see

Top Sights	p24
Sights	p28
Eating	p29
Drinking	p31
Entertainment	p32
Shopping	p32

E
F
G
H
1
2
3
4
5
0 1 km
0 0.5 miles
Wave Organ
5
Marina Green
Yacht Rd
Yacht Harbor
Marina Green Dr
Marina Blvd
Fort Mason Center
16
7
4
22
12
17
Fort Mason
Mason St
Jefferson St
Beach St
Cervantes Blvd
Fillmore St
Laguna St
Bay St
Palace Dr
101
Palace of Fine Arts
3
North Point St
Avila St
Pierce St
George R Moscone Recreation Center
Francisco St
Chestnut St
Gorgas Ave
Baker St
Richardson Ave
Kennedy Ave
Presidio National Park
9
10
14
6
Lombard St
Octavia St
Presidio Blvd
Greenwich St
15
COW HOLLOW
Lombard St
Filbert St
21
Lyon St
Broderick St
Divisadero St
Union St
13
18
20
19
Buchanan St
Webster St
Green St
Clarke St
Presidio Blvd
Lyon Steps
Vallejo St
Scott St
Steiner St
Broadway
Pacific Ave
Jackson St
Pacific Ave
Washington St
PACIFIC HEIGHTS
Alta Plaza Park
University of the Pacific
Clay St
Sacramento St
California St
Pine St
Presidio Ave

Sights

Crissy Field

PARK

1 Map p26, D2

War is for the birds at Crissy Field, a military airstrip turned waterfront nature preserve with knockout Golden Gate views. Where military aircraft once zoomed in for landings, bird-watchers now huddle in the silent rushes of a reclaimed tidal marsh. Joggers pound beachside trails and the only security alerts are raised by puppies suspiciously sniffing surfers. On foggy days, stop by the certified-green Warming Hut (p30) to browse regional-nature books and warm up with fair-trade coffee. (415-561-4700; www.crissyfield.org; 1199 East Beach; P; 30, PresidiGo Shuttle)

Baker Beach

BEACH

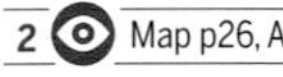

2 Map p26, A3

Picnic amid wind-sculpted pines, fish from craggy rocks or frolic nude at mile-long Baker Beach, with spectacular views of the Golden Gate. Crowds come weekends, especially on fog-free days; arrive early. For nude sunbathing (mostly straight girls and gay boys), head to the north. Families in clothing stick to the south, nearer parking. Mind the currents and the c-c-cold water. (10am-5pm 415-561-4323; www.nps.gov/prsf; sunrise-sunset; P; 29, PresidiGo Shuttle)

Palace of Fine Arts

MONUMENT

3 Map p26, E3

Like a fossilized party favor, this romantic, ersatz Greco-Roman ruin is the city's memento from the 1915 Panama-Pacific International Exposition. The original, designed by celebrated Berkeley architect Bernard Maybeck, was of wood, burlap and plaster, then later reinforced. By the 1960s it was crumbling. The structure was recast in concrete so that future generations could gaze at the rotunda relief to glimpse 'Art under attack by materialists, with idealists leaping to her rescue.' A glorious spot to wander day or night. (510-599-4651; www.lovethepalace.org; Palace Dr; admission free; 24hr; 28, 30, 43)

Fort Mason Center

AREA

4 Map p26, H2

San Francisco takes subversive glee in turning military installations into venues for nature, fine dining and out-there experimental art. Evidence: Fort Mason, once a shipyard and embarkation point for WWII troops, now a vast cultural center and gathering place for events, drinking and eating. Wander the waterfront, keeping your eyes peeled for fascinating outdoor art-and-science installations designed by the Exploratorium (p50). (415-345-7500; www.fortmason.org; cnr Marina Blvd & Laguna St; P; 22, 28, 30, 43, 47, 49)

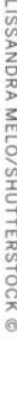

Palace of Fine Arts

Wave Organ

MONUMENT

5 Map p26, G2

A project of the Exploratorium, the Wave Organ is a sound sculpture of PVC tubes and concrete pipes capped with found marble from San Francisco's old cemetery, built into the tip of the yacht-harbor jetty. Depending on the waves, winds and tide, the tones emitted sound like nervous humming from a dinnertime line cook or spooky heavy breathing over the phone in a slasher film. (www.exploratorium.edu/visit/wave-organ; Marina Small Craft Harbor jetty; admission free; daylight hours; ; 22, 30)

Eating

A16

ITALIAN **$$$**

6  Map p26, F3

Even before A16 won a James Beard Award, it was hard to book, but persevere: the housemade mozzarella *burrata*, blister-crusted pizzas from the wood-burning oven and 12-page Italian wine list make it worth your while. Skip the spotty desserts and instead double up on adventurous appetizers, including house-cured *salumi* platters and delectable marinated tuna. (415-771-2216; www.a16pizza.com; 2355 Chestnut St; pizzas $18-21, mains $22-36; lunch 11:30am-2:30pm Wed-Sun, dinner

Local Life

Off the Grid Food Trucks

On Friday nights spring through fall, some 30 **food trucks** (Map p26, H2; www.offthegridsf.com; Fort Mason Center, 2 Marina Blvd; items $6-14; 5-10pm Fri Apr-Oct; ; 22, 28) circle their wagons at SF's largest mobile-gourmet hootenannies. Arrive early for the best selection and to minimize waits. Cash only.

These weekly parties are a great way to appreciate the breadth of the SF food scene while rubbing elbows with locals. Some favorites: clamshell buns stuffed with duck and mango from the **Chairman**, free-range herbed roast chicken from **Roli Roti** and, on Friday, pizza and meatballs from **A16** (p29).

5:30-10pm Mon-Thu, 5-11pm Fri & Sat, 5-10pm Sun; 28, 30, 43)

Greens VEGETARIAN, CALIFORNIAN $$

7  Map p26, H2

Career carnivores won't realize there's zero meat in the hearty black-bean chili, or in Greens' other vegetarian dishes, made using ingredients from a Zen farm. And, oh, what views! The Golden Gate rises just outside the window-lined dining room. The on-site cafe serves to-go lunches, but for sit-down meals reservations are essential. (415-771-6222; www.greensrestaurant.com; Fort Mason Center, 2 Marina Blvd, Bldg A; mains lunch $16-19, dinner $20-28; 11:45am-2:30pm & 5:30-9pm; ; 22, 28, 30, 43, 47, 49)

Warming Hut CAFE $

8  Map p26, B2

At the Warming Hut, wet-suited windsurfers and Crissy Field kite fliers recharge with fair-trade coffee, organic pastries and hot dogs while browsing field guides and sampling honey from Presidio honeybees. Ingeniously insulated with recycled denim, this eco-shack below the Golden Gate Bridge evolved from a heartwarming concept: all purchases fund Crissy Field's ongoing conversion from US Army airstrip to wildlife preserve. (415-561-3042; www.parksconservancy.org/visit/eat/warming-hut.html; 983 Marine Dr; items $4-9; 9am-5pm; P; PresidiGo shuttle)

Lucca Delicatessen DELI $

9 Map p26, G3

Open since 1929, this classic Italian deli is an ideal spot to assemble picnics for Marina Green. Expect made-to-order sandwiches on fresh-baked Acme bread, including yummy meatball subs. There's hot homemade soup from 11am to 3pm. (415-921-7873; www.luccadeli.com; 2120 Chestnut St; sandwiches $9-12; 9am-6pm; 28, 30, 43)

Blue Barn Gourmet SANDWICHES $

10  Map p26, G3

For $12.95, build a mighty mound of organic produce, topped with six fixings, including artisan cheeses, caramelized onions, heirloom tomatoes, candied pecans and

pomegranate seeds. For something hot, try the grilled cheese with *soppressata* salami, *manchego* cheese and Mission-fig jam. On balmy days, sit on the back patio. (415-896-4866; www.bluebarngourmet.com; 3344 Steiner St; salads & sandwiches $11-16; 11am-8:30pm Mon-Fri, to 8pm Sat & Sun; 22, 28, 30, 43)

Arguello MEXICAN $$

11 Map p26, D4

Inside the Presidio Officers' Club, this lively Mexican restaurant by James Beard Award–winner Traci Des Jardins features small dishes good for sharing, plus several mains, including standout caramelized pork shoulder. The bar makes great margaritas, which you can sip fireside in the adjoining Moraga Hall, the former officers'-club lounge. (415-561-3650; www.arguellosf.com; 50 Moraga Ave; mains $18-25; 11am-4pm Tue, to 9pm Wed-Fri, 11am-3pm & 5-9pm Sat, 11am-4pm Sun; ; 43, PresidiGo shuttle)

Drinking

Interval Bar & Cafe BAR

12 Map p26, H2

The Interval is a favorite spot in the Marina for cocktails and philosophical conversations. It's inside the Long Now Foundation, with floor-to-ceiling bookshelves, which contain the canon of Western lit, rising above a glorious 10,000-year clock – a fitting backdrop for a daiquiri, gimlet or aged Tom Collins. (www.theinterval.org; Fort Mason Center, 2 Marina Blvd, Bldg A; 10am-midnight; 10, 22, 28, 30, 47, 49)

West Coast Wine & Cheese WINE BAR

13 Map p26, G4

A rack of 720 bottles frames the wall at this austerely elegant storefront wine bar, which pourswines exclusively from California, Oregon and Washington, 26 by the glass. All pair with delectable small bites (dishes $8 to $16), including house-made charcuterie and cheese plates. (www.westcoastsf.com; 2165 Union St; 4-10pm Mon & Tue, to 11pm Wed, to midnight Thu & Fri, 2pm-midnight Sat, to 10pm Sun; 22, 41, 45)

California Wine Merchant WINE BAR

14 Map p26, G3

Part wine store, part wine bar, this small shop on busy Chestnut St caters to neighborhood wine aficionados, with a daily-changing list of 50 wines by the glass, available in half pours. Arrive early to score a seat, or stand and gab with the locals. (415-567-1639; www.californiawinemerchant.com; 2113 Chestnut St; 11am-midnight Mon-Wed, to 1:30am Thu-Sat, to 11pm Sun; 22, 30, 43)

MatrixFillmore LOUNGE

15 Map p26, G3

The neighborhood's most notorious upmarket pick-up joint provides a

fascinating glimpse of the lives of single Marina swankers. Treat it as a comic sociological study, while enjoying stellar cocktails and sexy beats – if, that is, you can get past the door. There's dancing after 10pm. Bring your credit card. (415-598-9222; www.matrixfillmore.com; 3138 Fillmore St; 5pm-2am Wed-Sun; 22, 28, 30, 43)

Entertainment

Magic Theatre

THEATER

16 Map p26, H2

The Magic is known for taking risks and staging provocative plays by playwrights such as Bill Pullman, Terrence McNally, Edna O'Brien, David Mamet and longtime playwright-in-residence Sam Shepard. If you're interested in seeing new theatrical works and getting under the skin of the Bay Area theater scene, the Magic is an excellent starting point. Check the calendar online. (415-441-8822; www.magictheatre.org; Fort Mason Center, cnr Marina Blvd & Laguna St, Bldg D, 3rd fl; tickets $30-85; 22, 28, 30, 43, 47, 49)

BATS Improv

THEATER

17 Map p26, H2

Bay Area Theater Sports explores all things improv, from audience-inspired themes to whacked-out musicals at completely extemporaneous weekend shows. Or take center stage yourself at a three-hour improv-comedy workshop (held weekday nights and weekend afternoons). Think fast: classes fill quickly. Admission prices vary depending on the show/workshop. (415-474-8935; www.improv.org; Fort Mason Center, cnr Marina Blvd & Laguna St, Bldg B, 3rd fl; $17-20; shows 8pm Fri & Sat; 22, 28, 30, 43)

Shopping

ATYS

HOMEWARES

18 Map p26, G4

Tucked in a courtyard, this design showcase is like a museum store for exceptional, artistic household items – to wit, a mirrored coat rack, a rechargeable flashlight that turns a wineglass into a lamp, and a zero-emissions, solar-powered toy airplane. Expect sleek, modern designs of superior quality that you won't find anywhere else. (415-441-9220; www.atysdesign.com; 2149b Union St; 11am-6:30pm Mon-Sat, noon-6pm Sun; 22, 41, 45)

Epicurean Trader

FOOD & DRINKS

19 Map p26, H4

A must-visit for discerning bartenders, this grocery, liquor store and deli carries only small-batch products, many locally made, with an emphasis on bar supplies – grass-flavored gin with elderflower tonic, anyone? The deli makes perfect paninis on bread from Tartine; for dessert there's Humphry Slocombe ice cream by the scoop.

(☎415-780-1628; www.theepicureantrader.com; 1909 Union St; ⊙10am-9pm Sun-Tue, to 10pm Wed-Sat; 🚌22, 41, 45, 47, 49)

Sui Generis Illa

CLOTHING

20 Map p26, H4

Sui generis is Latin for one of a kind – which is what you'll find at this high-end designer consignment shop that features recent seasons' looks, one-of-a-kind gowns and a few archival pieces by key couturiers from decades past. No jeans, no pants – unless they're leather or superglam. Yes, it's pricey, but far cheaper than you'd pay shopping retail. (☎415-800-4584; www.suigenerisconsignment.com; 2147 Union St; ⊙11am-7pm Mon-Sat, to 5pm Sun; 🚌22, 41, 45)

My Roommate's Closet

CLOTHING

21 Map p26, G4

All the half-off bargains and none of the clawing dangers of a sample sale. Stocks constantly change but have included cloud-like Catherine Malandrino chiffon party dresses, executive Diane von Furstenberg wrap dresses and designer denim at prices approaching reality. (☎415-447-7703; www.shopmrc.com; 3044 Fillmore St; ⊙11am-7pm Mon-Sat, noon-6pm Sun; 🚌22, 41, 45)

Wave Organ (p29) © Exploratorium, www.exploratorium.edu

Flax Art & Design

DESIGN

22 Map p26, H2

The city's finest art-supply store carries a dizzying array of ink, paints, pigment, brushes, pens, pencils, markers, glues and gums, plus paper in myriad varieties, from stationery and wrapping to drawing pads and sketch tablets. If you're a serious designer or artist, Flax is a must-visit. (☎415-530-3510; http://flaxart.com; 2 Marina Blvd, Bldg D; ⊙10am-6:30pm Mon-Sat, to 6pm Sun; 🚌22, 28, 30, 43)

Explore

Fisherman's Wharf & the Piers

The waterfront that today welcomes families fresh off the boat from Alcatraz tours was a dodgy dock area during California's Gold Rush. After the 1906 earthquake and fire, a retaining wall was built, and Sunday strollers gradually replaced drifters and grifters along Embarcadero boardwalks. But Wild West manners prevail on Pier 39, where sea lions snore and belch like drunken sailors dockside.

The Sights in a Day

Escapees from Alcatraz flee the piers fast – but families might be held captive by Pier 39's kid-friendly attractions, especially **Aquarium of the Bay** (p38) and **San Francisco Carousel** (p39). Otherwise, salute Pier 39's resident **sea lions** (p37) dockside, and race boardwalk crowds to an early lunch at **Codmother Fish & Chips** (p44).

Recover from the inevitable starch stupor by saving the world from Space Invaders and playing steampunk arcade games at **Musée Mécanique** (p37), then enter stealth mode on an actual WWII submarine: the **USS Pampanito** (p37). Back on dry land, explore 1930s murals inside the shipshape **Maritime Museum** (p41) and warm up with Irish coffee at **Buena Vista Cafe** (p46). Hop off the Hyde St cable car at wiggly **Lombard Street** (p41) for poetry-inspiring Golden Gate vistas, and glimpse a master muralist at work in the San Francisco fresco-within-a-fresco at **Diego Rivera Gallery** (p42).

For dinner, go high or low: **Gary Danko** (p43) for award-winning California cuisine or fast food at **In-N-Out Burger** (p44).

Top Sight

Fisherman's Wharf

Best of San Francisco

Freebies

Maritime Museum (p41)

Sea Lions at Pier 39 (p37)

For Kids

Musée Mécanique (p37)

Sea Lions at Pier 39 (p37)

Aquarium of the Bay (p38)

Eating Out

Gary Danko (p43)

Museums & Galleries

USS Pampanito (p37)

Maritime Museum (p41)

Getting There

M **Streetcar** Historic F Market streetcars connect the Wharf with the Castro via downtown.

Cable car The Powell-Hyde and Powell-Mason lines run up Powell St to the Wharf.

Bus Wharf–downtown buses include 30, 47 and 49.

Car Park at public garages at Pier 39 and Ghirardelli Sq.

Top Sights
Fisherman's Wharf

Where fishermen once snared sea creatures, San Francisco now traps tourists in a commercial sprawl between the cable-car terminus and the Alcatraz Cruises port. But where you'd least expect it, Fisherman's Wharf offers surprise and delight. Here you can sunbathe with sea lions, ride carousel unicorns, experience stealth mode inside a WWII submarine, consult 100-year-old fortune-tellers, and watch sharks circle from the safety of glass tubes built right into the bay.

Map p40, C2

www.fishermanswharf.org

19, 30, 47, 49, Powell-Mason, Powell-Hyde, M F

Sea lions at Fisherman's Wharf

Sea Lions at Pier 39

Rock stars wish they could live like San Francisco's sea lions, who've taken over an entire yacht marina with their harems since 1990. Since California law requires boats to make way for marine mammals, up to 1300 sea-lion squatters oblige yacht-owners to relinquish **Pier 39** (415-705-5500; www.pier39.com; cnr Beach St & the Embarcadero; P; 47, Powell-Mason, M E, F) slips from January through July. Night and day they canoodle, belch, scratch and gleefully shove one another off the docks.

Musée Mécanique

Laughing Sal has freaked out visitors with her coin-operated cackle for 100 years, but don't let this manic mannequin deter you from the best arcade in the west. With a few quarters at the **Musée Mécanique** (415-346-2000; www.museemechanique.org; Pier 45, Shed A; 10am-8pm; ; 47, Powell-Mason, Powell-Hyde, M E, F), you can start bar brawls in mechanical Wild West saloons, save the world from Space Invaders and get your fortune told by an eerily lifelike wooden swami.

USS Pampanito

Dive, dive, dive! Head into the belly of a restored **WWII US Navy submarine** (415-775-1943, tickets 855-384-6410; www.maritime.org/pamphome.htm; Pier 45; adult/child/family $20/10/45; 9am-8pm Thu-Tue, to 6pm Wed; ; 19, 30, 47, Powell-Hyde, M E, F) that sunk six Japanese ships (including two carrying British and Australian POWs). Submariners' stories of tense moments in underwater stealth mode will have you holding your breath – caution, claustrophobes – and all those brass knobs and hydraulic valves make 21st-century technology seem overrated.

Top Tips

- Afternoon fog blows in around 4pm, sometimes earlier in summer. Carry a jacket and don't wear shorts, except in a rare heatwave.
- Most people cover waterfront attractions on foot or bike – wear comfortable shoes and sunscreen.
- Fisherman's Wharf is most popular with families, who pack the waterfront by early afternoon. To dodge the crowds, arrive at Pier 43½ seafood shacks early for lunch and visit the USS *Pampanito* and Maritime Museum in the afternoon.

Take a Break

Snack shacks line the Pier 39 boardwalk and flank picnic benches at Pier 43½, including Fisherman's Wharf Crab Stands (p44). To treat/bribe kids, try Kara's Cupcakes (p45).

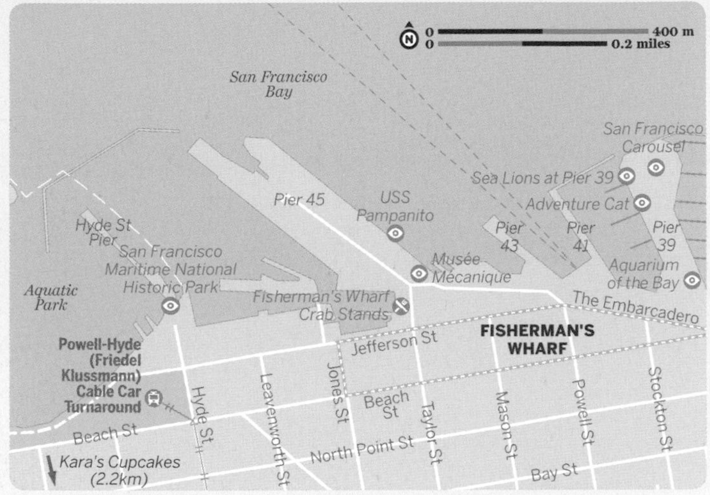

Aquarium of the Bay

Take a long walk off a short pier right into the bay, and stay perfectly safe and dry as sharks circle, manta rays flutter and schools of fish flit overhead. The **aquarium** (☎415-623-5300; www.aquariumofthebay.org; Pier 39; adult/child/family $24.95/14.95/70; ⏱9am-8pm late May-early Sep, shorter hours low season; 👪; 🚌49, 🚋Powell-Mason, Ⓜ E, F) is built into the bay, with a conveyor belt transporting you through underwater glass tubes for an up-close look at local aquaculture.

Maritime National Historical Park

'Aye, she's a beauty,' you'll growl like a salty dog aboard **historic ships** (☎415-447-5000; www.nps.gov/safr; 499 Jefferson St, Hyde St Pier; 7-day ticket adult/child $10/free; ⏱9:30am-5pm Oct-May, to 5:30pm Jun-Sep; 👪; 🚌19, 30, 47, 🚋Powell-Hyde, Ⓜ F) open as museums along Hyde St Pier – especially elegant 1891 schooner *Alma* and iconic 1890 steamboat *Eureka*. Other boats resemble giant bath toys, including steam-powered paddle-wheel tugboat *Eppleton Hall* and triple-masted, iron-hulled 1886 British *Balclutha*, which hauled coal to San Francisco via Cape Horn.

San Francisco Carousel, Pier 39

San Francisco Carousel

Your chariot awaits to whisk you and the kids past the Golden Gate Bridge, Alcatraz and other SF landmarks hand-painted onto this Italian **carousel** (www.pier39.com; Pier 39; rides $3; 11am-7pm; ; 47, Powell-Mason, M E, F), twinkling with 1800 lights. Old-timey organ carnival music inspires goofy sing-alongs on the four-minute ride.

Adventure Cat

Centuries of sailors are right: there's no better view of San Francisco than from its silvery bay, especially on a sunset sail. **Adventure Cat** (415-777-1630; www.adventurecat.com; Pier 39; adult/child $45/25, sunset cruise $60; ; 47, M E, F) lets you sail off into the sunset on catamaran cruises with dazzling bay views, trampolines between hulls for bouncy kids and windless cabins in case of fog (dress warmly). Three daily cruises depart March to October; weekends only in November.

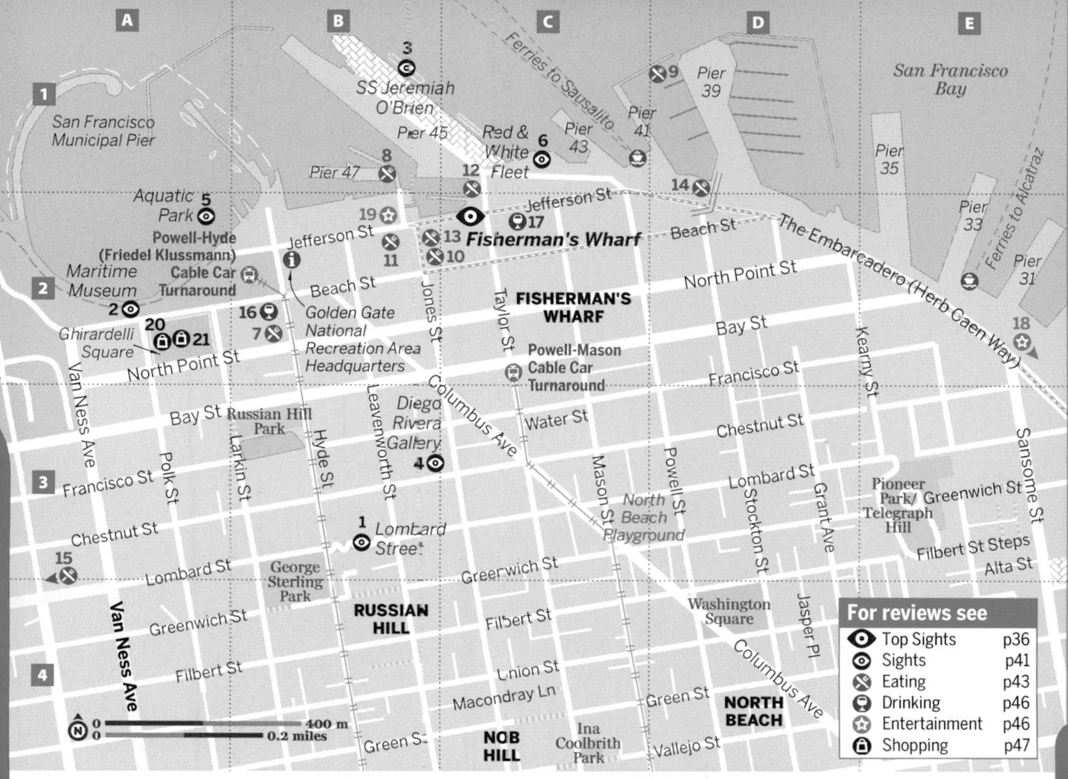
San Francisco Bay
Ferries to Alcatraz
Ferries to Sausalito
Pier 31
Pier 33
Pier 35
Pier 39
Pier 41
Pier 43
Pier 45
Pier 47
San Francisco Municipal Pier
SS Jeremiah O'Brien
Red & White Fleet
Fisherman's Wharf
FISHERMAN'S WHARF
Powell-Mason Cable Car Turnaround
Powell-Hyde (Friedel Klussmann) Cable Car Turnaround
Aquatic Park
Maritime Museum
Ghirardelli Square
Golden Gate National Recreation Area Headquarters
Diego Rivera Gallery
Lombard Street
Russian Hill Park
George Sterling Park
RUSSIAN HILL
NOB HILL
NORTH BEACH
North Beach Playground
Washington Square
Pioneer Park/Telegraph Hill
Ina Coolbrith Park
The Embarcadero (Herb Caen Way)
Jefferson St
Beach St
North Point St
Bay St
Francisco St
Chestnut St
Lombard St
Greenwich St
Filbert St
Filbert St Steps
Alta St
Union St
Macondray Ln
Green St
Vallejo St
Water St
Columbus Ave
Van Ness Ave
Polk St
Larkin St
Hyde St
Leavenworth St
Jones St
Taylor St
Mason St
Powell St
Stockton St
Grant Ave
Jasper Pl
Kearny St
Sansome St
For reviews see
Top Sights p36
Sights p41
Eating p43
Drinking p46
Entertainment p46
Shopping p47
400 m
0.2 miles

Lombard St

Sights

Lombard Street

STREET

1 Map p40, B3

You've seen the eight switchbacks of Lombard St's 900 block in a thousand photographs. The tourist board has dubbed it 'the world's crookedest street,' which is factually incorrect: Vermont St in Potrero Hill deserves that award, but Lombard is much more scenic, with its redbrick pavement and lovingly tended flowerbeds. It wasn't always so bent; before the arrival of the car it lunged straight down the hill. (Powell-Hyde)

Maritime Museum

MUSEUM

2 Map p40, A2

A monumental hint to sailors in need of a scrub, this restored, ship-shaped 1939 Streamline Moderne landmark is decked out with Works Progress Administration (WPA) art treasures: playful seal and frog sculptures by Beniamino Bufano, Hilaire Hiler's surreal underwater dreamscape murals, and recently uncovered wood reliefs by Richard Ayer. Acclaimed African American artist Sargent Johnson created the stunning carved green slate marquee doorway and the veranda's mesmerizing aquatic mosaics. (Aquatic Park Bathhouse; www.maritime.org; 900 Beach St; admission free; 10am-4pm; ; 19, 30, 47, Powell-Hyde)

Understand

The Left Coast

San Francisco's port thrived in 1934, but local longshoremen pulling long hours unloading heavy cargo for scant pay didn't see the upside of the shipping boom. When they protested dangerous working conditions, shipping tycoons sought dockworkers elsewhere – only to discover San Francisco's longshoremen had coordinated their strike with 35,000 workers along the West Coast. After 83 days, police and the National Guard broke the strike, killing 34 strikers and wounding 40 sympathizers. Public sympathy forced concessions from shipping magnates, and 1930s murals by Diego Rivera and Works Project Administration (WPA) artists reflect the pro-worker sentiment that swept the city known henceforth as America's 'Left Coast.'

SS Jeremiah O'Brien SHIP

3 Map p40, B1

It's hard to believe that this 10,000-ton beauty was turned out by San Francisco's shipbuilders in under eight weeks, and harder still to imagine how she dodged U-boats on a mission to deliver supplies to Allied forces on D-day. Of 2710 Liberty ships launched during WWII, this is the only one still fully operational. For steamy piston-on-piston, 2700HP action, visit during 'steaming weekends' (usually the third weekend of the month in summer) or check the website for upcoming four-hour cruises. (415-554-0100; www.ssjeremiahobrien.org; Pier 45; adult/child/family $20/10/40; 9am-4pm; ; 19, 30, 47, Powell-Hyde, M E, F)

Diego Rivera Gallery GALLERY

4 Map p40, B3

Diego Rivera's 1931 *The Making of a Fresco Showing the Building of a City* is a trompe l'oeil fresco within a fresco, showing the artist himself, pausing to admire his work, as well as the work in progress that is San Francisco. The fresco covers an entire wall in the Diego Rivera Gallery at the San Francisco Art Institute. For a memorable San Francisco aspect, head to the terrace cafe for espresso and panoramic bay views. (415-771-7020; www.sfai.edu; 800 Chestnut St; admission free; 9am-7pm; 30, Powell-Mason)

Aquatic Park PARK

5 Map p40, A2

Everyone loves this easy-access cove at Van Ness Ave's northern end, flanked by the massive comma-shaped Municipal Pier, where fishermen cast

their lines and lovers wander hand in hand. Eccentricity along Fisherman's Wharf is mostly staged, but here it's real: extreme swimmers dive from the concrete beachfront into the blood-curdling waters of the wintertime bay, eccentrics mumble conspiracy theories on the grassy knoll of panoramic Victoria Park, and wistful tycoons stare into the distance and contemplate sailing far away from their smartphones. (415-561-7000; www.nps.gov/safr; admission free; ; 19, 30, 47, Powell-Hyde)

Red & White Fleet

CRUISE

6 Map p40, C1

A one-hour bay cruise with Red & White lets you see the Golden Gate Bridge from the water. Brave the wind and sit on the outdoor upper deck. Audio tours in multiple languages provide narrative. On-board alcohol subdues naysayers. (415-673-2900; www.redandwhite.com; Pier 43½; adult/child $38/26; ; 47, M E, F)

Eating

Gary Danko

CALIFORNIAN **$$$**

7 Map p40, B2

Gary Danko wins James Beard Awards for his impeccable Californian *haute cuisine*. Smoked-glass windows prevent passersby from tripping over their tongues at the exquisite presentations – roasted lobster with blood oranges, blushing duck breast with port-roasted grapes, lavish cheeses and trios of crèmes brûlées. Reservations a must. (415-749-2060; www.garydanko.com; 800 North Point St; 3-/5-course menu $86/124; 5:30-10pm; 19, 30, 47, Powell-Hyde)

Scoma's

SEAFOOD **$$$**

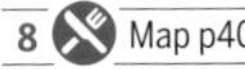

8 Map p40, B1

Enjoy a flashback to the 1960s, with waiters in white dinner jackets, pine-paneled walls decorated with signed photographs of forgotten celebrities, and plate-glass windows overlooking the docks – Scoma's is the Wharf's long-standing staple for seafood. Little changes, except the prices. Expect classics like *cioppino* (seafood stew) and lobster thermidor – never ground-breaking, always good – that taste better when someone else buys.

The restaurant accepts limited reservations but always accommodates walk-ins and has a retro-cool cocktail lounge where you can wait for your table. (415-771-4383; www.scomas.com; Pier 47; mains $28-40; 11:30am-9:30pm; P; Powell-Hyde, M F)

Forbes Island

GRILL **$$$**

9 Map p40, D1

No man is an island, except for an eccentric millionaire named Forbes Thor Kiddoo. A miniature lighthouse, a thatched hut, a waterfall, a sandy beach and swaying palms transformed his moored houseboat into the Hearst Castle of the bay. Today this bizarre domicile is a gently rocking, romantic

restaurant, strong on grilled meats and atmosphere – consider the lamb. Reservations essential. (415-951-4900; www.forbesisland.com; Pier 41; 4-course menu $79; 5pm-late; ; 47, MF)

Codmother Fish & Chips
FOOD TRUCK $

10 Map p40, B2

If being at Fisherman's Wharf makes you crave fish and chips, skip the expensive restaurants lining the water and instead find this little food truck, which makes delicious fried cod, Baja-style fish tacos and several varieties of flavored French fries. Note the early closing times. (415-606-9349; 2824 Jones St; mains $5-10; 11:30am-5pm Mon & Wed-Sat, to 2:30pm Sun; 47, Powell-Mason, MF)

Top Tip

Sourdough Bread

San Francisco's climate isn't great for swimsuits, but it's perfect for *Lactobacillus sanfranciscensis,* the lactic-acid bacteria that gives sourdough bread its distinctive tang and helps activate yeast. Any self-respecting San Francisco bakery serves sourdough, but the most famous is **Boudin Bakery** (Map p40, C2; www.boudinbakery.com; 160 Jefferson St; items $8-16; 11am-9:30pm; 47, MF), a San Francisco institution since 1849.

In-N-Out Burger
BURGERS $

11 Map p40, B2

Gourmet burgers have taken SF by storm, but In-N-Out has had a good thing going for 60 years: prime chuck beef processed on site, plus fries and shakes made with ingredients you can pronounce, all served by employees paid a living wage. Consider ordering yours off the menu 'Animal style,' cooked in mustard with grilled onions. (800-786-1000; www.in-n-out.com; 333 Jefferson St; meals under $10; 10:30am-1am Sun-Thu, to 1:30am Fri & Sat; ; 30, 47, Powell-Hyde)

Fisherman's Wharf Crab Stands
SEAFOOD $

12 Map p40, C1

Brawny men stir steaming cauldrons of Dungeness crab at several side-by-side takeout crab stands at the foot of Taylor St, the epicenter of Fisherman's Wharf. Crab season typically runs winter through spring, but you'll find shrimp and other seafood year-round. (Taylor St; mains $5-15; MF)

Carmel Pizza Co
FOOD TRUCK $$

13 Map p40, B2

It's remarkable that a food truck could contain a wood-burning oven, but herein lies the secret to Carmel's remarkably good single-serving blistered-crust pizzas. Note the early closing time at dinner. (415-676-1185; www.carmelpizzaco.com; 2826 Jones St; pizzas $13-21; 11:30am-3:30pm & 5-8pm Mon,

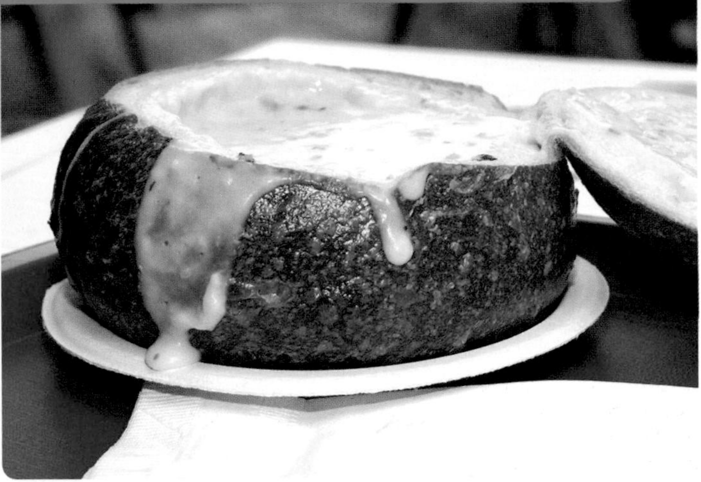

Clam chowder served in a bread bowl

Tue & Thu, noon-8pm Fri & Sat, to 6pm Sun; 47, Powell-Mason, MF)

Eagle Cafe AMERICAN $$

14  Map p40, D1

Good for breakfast or a no-fuss lunch, the Eagle's straightforward fare includes pancakes and omelets, crab-salad sandwiches, burgers etc. The views are good, the prices are right for families and it takes reservations, which you should definitely make at weekends to spare yourself (long) waits. (415-433-3689; www.eaglecafe.com; Pier 39, 2nd fl, suite 103; mains $10-20; 7:30am-9pm; ; 47, Powell-Mason, MF)

Kara's Cupcakes BAKERY, DESSERTS $

15 Map p40, A3

Proustian nostalgia washes over fully grown adults as they bite into cupcakes that recall childhood magician-led birthday parties. Varieties range from yummy chocolate marshmallow to classic carrot cake with cream-cheese frosting, all meticulously calculated for maximum glee – there's even gluten-free. (415-563-2253; www.karascupcakes.com; 3249 Scott St; cupcakes $2-3.75; 10am-8pm Sun-Thu, to 10pm Fri & Sat; 28, 30, 43)

Drinking

Buena Vista Cafe

BAR

16 Map p40, B2

Warm your cockles with a prim little goblet of bitter-creamy Irish coffee, introduced to America at this destination bar that once served sailors and cannery workers. That old Victorian floor manages to hold up carousers and families alike, served community-style at round tables overlooking the cable-car turnaround at Victoria Park. (415-474-5044; www.thebuenavista.com; 2765 Hyde St; 9am-2am Mon-Fri, 8am-2am Sat & Sun; ; 19, 47, Powell-Hyde)

Top Tip

Blazing Saddles

To gear up for a Gary Danko feast, cover the waterfront from Pier 39 to the Golden Gate Bridge on a rental bicycle. Besides the main shop on Hyde St, **Blazing Saddles** (Map p40, B2; 415-202-8888; www.blazingsaddles.com/san-francisco; 2715 Hyde St; bicycle rental per hour $8-15, per day $32-88, electric bikes per day $48-88; 8am-8pm; ; Powell-Hyde) has six rental stands around Fisherman's Wharf, and offers electric bikes and 24-hour return service. Reserve online for a 10% discount; rentals include all extras (helmets, bungee cords, packs etc).

Gold Dust Lounge

BAR

17 Map p40, C2

The Gold Dust is so beloved by San Franciscans that, when it lost its lease on the Union Sq building it had occupied since the 1930s, then reopened in 2013 at the Wharf – with the same precarious Victorian brass chandeliers and twangy rockabilly band – the mayor declared it 'Gold Dust Lounge Day.' (415-397-1695; www.golddustsf.com; 165 Jefferson St; 9am-2am; 47, Powell-Mason, M E, F)

Entertainment

Pier 23

LIVE MUSIC

18 Map p40, E2

It resembles a surf shack, but this old waterfront restaurant regularly features R&B, reggae, Latin bands, mellow rock and the occasional jazz pianist – and most shows are free. Wander out to the bayside patio to soak in the views. The dinner menu features pier-worthy options like batter-fried oysters and whole roasted crab. (415-362-5125; www.pier23cafe.com; Pier 23; cover free-$10; shows 5-7pm Tue, 6-8pm Wed, 7-10pm Thu-Sat, 5-8pm Sun; M E, F)

Lou's Fish Shack

LIVE MUSIC

19  Map p40, B2

Lou's presents live blues on Friday and Saturday nights and Sunday afternoons. Primarily a restaurant, it also has a few bar tables near the bandstand and a tiny

CYNTHIA LIANG/SHUTTERSTOCK ©

Crab sculpture by topiary artist Jeff Brees

dance floor, making it a good backup when you're staying nearby and want to hear live music but don't want to travel. And, unlike bona fide blues bars, Lou's welcomes kids. (☎415-771-5687; http://lousfishshacksf.com; 300 Jefferson St; admission free; ⏰shows 7-11pm Fri & Sat, 4-8pm Sun; 👪; 🚌30, 47, 🚋Powell-Mason, Ⓜ F)

Shopping

elizabethW PERFUME

20 🛍 Map p40, A2

Local scent maker elizabethW supplies the tantalizing aromas of changing seasons without the sweaty brows or frozen toes. 'Sweet Tea' smells like a Georgia porch in summertime, 'Vetiver' like autumn in Maine. For a true SF fragrance, 'Leaves' is as audaciously green as Golden Gate Park in January. (☎415-441-8354; www.elizabethw.com; 900 North Point St; ⏰10am-6pm Mon-Thu, to 9pm Fri & Sat, to 8pm Sun; 🚌19, 30, 47, 🚋Powell-Hyde)

Helpers Bazaar VINTAGE

21 🛍 Map p40, A2

Socialite and philanthropist Joy Venturini Bianchi operates this 100%-for-charity boutique, where, if you dig, you may find Chanel. If not, there's always costume jewelry and Christmas ornaments. (☎415-441-0779; Ghirardelli Sq, Plaza Bldg; ⏰10am-9pm Mon-Sat, to 6pm Sun; 🚌19, 30, 47, 49, 🚋Powell-Hyde)

Top Sights
Alcatraz

Getting There

Ferry An Alcatraz Cruises ferry is the only way to reach the island. You must reserve a specific departure time – book at least a week ahead for the best choice.

Enter a D-Block solitary cell, shut the iron door and listen carefully: beyond these bars and across the bay, you can hear the murmur of everyday life. Now you understand the peculiar torment of America's most notorious prison – and why inmates risked riptides to escape from Alcatraz. Day visits include captivating audio tours with prisoners and guards recalling cell-house life, while creepy twilight tours are led by park rangers. On the boat back to San Francisco, freedom never felt so good.

Alcatraz

Cell Block

In 1934 America's first military prison became a maximum-security cell block housing most-wanted criminals, from crime boss Al Capone to Soviet spy Morton Sobell. Though Alcatraz was considered escape-proof, in 1962 the Anglin brothers and Frank Morris floated away on a makeshift raft and were never seen again. Their escape plot is showcased on the fascinating cell-block tour, which also covers riots, censorship and solitary confinement.

Native American Landmarks

In the 19th century, Alcatraz was a military prison holding Civil War deserters and Native American 'unfriendlies' – including 19 Hopi who refused to send their children to government boarding schools where Hopi language and religion were forbidden. After the prison was closed in 1963, activists petitioned to turn Alcatraz into a Native American study center – but the federal government refused. Native American leaders occupied the island in 1969 in protest, and their 19-month standoff with the FBI is commemorated in a dockside museum and 'This Is Indian Land' graffiti.

Nature Trails

After the government regained control of Alcatraz, it became a national park. By 1973 it had already become a major draw for visitors and the namesake birds of Isla de Alcatraces (Isle of the Pelicans). Wear sturdy shoes to explore unpaved trails to the prison laundry area that has become a prime bird-watching zone, and glimpse native plants thriving in the ruins of prison-guard homes.

Alcatraz Cruises 415-981-7625

www.nps.gov/alcatraz

tours adult/child 5-11yr day $37.25/23, night $44.25/26.50

call center 8am-7pm, ferries depart Pier 33 half-hourly 8:45am-3:50pm, night tours 5:55pm & 6:30pm

Top Tips

- Book well ahead: a month for self-guided daytime visits, two to three months for night tours.
- It's often windy and much colder on Alcatraz, so wear extra layers, long pants and a cap.
- Book the day's first or last boat to avoid crowds. You need only reserve the outbound boat, not the return.

Take a Break

Most people spend three to four hours; bring lunch to linger longer. Note: eating is allowed only at the ferry dock. There's no food on the island, only bottled water, coffee and nuts.

Top Sights
Exploratorium

Getting There

M **Streetcar** Take the F line from the Wharf, downtown or the Castro. Get off at Embarcadero station, and walk four blocks north to Pier 15.

Hear salt sing, stimulate your appetite with color, and try on static-electricity punk hairdos with hands-on exhibits created by MacArthur Genius Grant winners. Manhattan Project nuclear physicist Frank Oppenheimer founded the Exploratorium in 1969 to explore science, art and human perception – and you can actually simulate '60s flashbacks as you grope barefoot through the Tactile Dome. The thrilling exhibits are matched by the setting: a 9-acre, glass-walled pier jutting over San Francisco Bay.

Exploratorium

Award-Winning Exhibits

Is there a science to skateboarding? Do toilets really flush counterclockwise in Australia? Find answers to questions you wished you'd learned in school, with 600-plus exhibits that have buttons to push, cranks to ratchet and dials to adjust. Peek into the in-house workshop to see artists and scientists inventing their next extreme science project.

Indoor Galleries

Indoor galleries focus on color, sound, light and motion, and educational photo ops abound: turn yourself into a human sundial, or get totally trippy in an optical-illusion room. Exploratorium exhibits are purpose-built to excite visitors with possibilities for new inventions, scientific discovery and public service – a fitting tribute to founder Frank Oppenheimer, an atom-bomb physicist who was blackballed during the McCarthy era, then later reemerged as a San Francisco high-school teacher.

Outdoor Gallery

San Francisco's weird-science showcase fills a 330,000-sq-ft solar-powered landmark on Pier 15, with vast outdoor portions you can explore for free, 24 hours a day. Listen to the wind play eerie compositions on the 27ft Aeolian harp, see the bay turn upside down in the Rickshaw Obscura and spot sensational Over the Water art installations.

Bay Observatory

With assistance from National Oceanic and Atmospheric Administration (NOAA), the Exploratorium's pier is wired with sensors delivering real-time data on weather, wind, tides and the bay. See the data flow at the glass-enclosed lookout of the Bay Observatory Gallery.

415-528-4444

www.exploratorium.edu

Pier 15

adult/child $30/20, 6-10pm Thu $15

10am-5pm Tue-Sun, over 18yr only 6-10pm Thu

P

Top Tips

- Make reservations, and plan your day around your visit.
- Don't miss the **Tactile Dome** (advance reservations and separate $15 ticket required), which challenges you to see with your other four senses.

Take a Break

When it's time to take a break, there's no need to leave the building – the on-site cafes are wonderful and there's not much else immediately nearby.

Explore

North Beach & Chinatown

Coffee or tea? East or west? You'll never have to decide in San Francisco, where historic Chinese and Italian neighborhoods are linked by poetry-lined Jack Kerouac Alley. Wander backstreets dotted with pagoda-topped temples and saloons where the Gold Rush, Chinese revolution and the Beat movement started. Rising above it all is Coit Tower, ringed by murals and jealously guarded by parrots.

The Sights in a Day

Start on Grant Ave, lined with pagoda-topped buildings purpose-built in the 1920s by Chinatown merchants to attract curiosity seekers and souvenir shoppers – clearly their plan worked like a charm. Hard to believe this cheerful vintage-neon-signed street was once a notorious red-light district – at least until you see the fascinating displays at the **Chinese Historical Society of America** (p58). Stop by **Tin How Temple** (p60) to admire the altar that miraculously survived the 1906 earthquake, and detour for dim sum at **City View** (p64).

Cross into North Beach via **Jack Kerouac Alley** (p60) and **City Lights** (p58), San Francisco's free-speech landmark. Espresso at **Caffe Trieste** (p65) turbocharges your North Beach walking tour, and speeds you up giddy, garden-lined Filbert St Steps to **Coit Tower** (p54).

Brave a Barbary Coast happy-hour crawl from **15 Romolo** (p66) to **Comstock Saloon** (p64) and **Tosca Cafe** (p62). San Franciscans will only excuse you from a final round at **Specs** (p64) for three reasons: reservations at **Coi** (p61), tickets to **Beach Blanket Babylon** (p66) or shows at **Bimbo's 365 Club** (p67).

Top Sight

Coit Tower & Filbert Steps (p54)

Best of San Francisco

Eating Out

Coi (p61)

Cotogna (p61)

Liguria Bakery (p62)

Z & Y (p62)

Drinks

Caffe Trieste (p65)

Comstock Saloon (p64)

Specs (p64)

Tosca Cafe (p62)

Shopping

City Lights Books (p58)

Golden Gate Fortune Cookie Company (p68)

Getting There

Cable car From downtown or the Wharf, take the Powell-Mason line through Chinatown and North Beach. The California St cable car passes through Chinatown.

Bus Key bus routes are 30, 41 and 45.

Top Sights
Coit Tower & Filbert Steps

The exclamation point on San Francisco's skyline is Coit Tower, built as a monument to firefighters by eccentric heiress Lillie Hitchcock Coit. This concrete projectile became a lightning rod for controversy for its provocative frescoes of San Francisco during the Great Depression – but no matter your perspective, the tower's viewing platform panoramas are breathtaking. The climb here along wooden Filbert Steps offers staggering adventure, with wild parrots squawking encouragement.

Map p56, D2

415-249-0995

www.coittowertours.com

Telegraph Hill Blvd

free, nonresident elevator fee adult/child $8/5

10am-6pm Apr-Oct, to 5pm Nov-Mar

39

Christopher Columbus statue by sculptor Vittorio di Colbertaldo. Collection of the City and County of San Francisco

WPA Murals

Coit Tower's Works Project Administration (WPA) murals show San Franciscans during the Great Depression, gathered at soup kitchens and dockworkers' unions, partying despite Prohibition, and poring over multilingual library books – including Marxist manifestos. These federally funded artworks proved controversial in 1934, and authorities denounced their 26 artists as communist – but San Franciscans embraced Coit Tower's bright, bold murals as beloved city landmarks.

Viewing Platform

After the 20-minute walk uphill to Coit Tower, the wait and admission fee to take the elevator to the top of the tower is well worth it. From the panoramic open-air platform 210ft above San Francisco, you can spot two bridges, cable cars and skyline-defining landmarks.

Filbert Street Steps

In the 19th century a ruthless entrepreneur began quarrying Telegraph Hill and blasting away roads – much to the distress of his neighbors. City Hall eventually stopped the quarrying of Telegraph Hill, but the views of the bay from garden-lined, cliffside Filbert St Steps are still (wait for it) dynamite.

Napier Lane

Along the steep climb from Sansome St up Filbert St Steps toward Coit Tower, stop for a breather along Napier Lane, a wooden boardwalk lined with cottages and gardens where wild parrots have flocked for decades.

Top Tips

- To see seven murals hidden inside Coit Tower's stairwell, take the free, docent-led tour at 11am on Wednesdays and Saturdays.
- For a bird's-eye view of San Francisco, don't miss the award-winning 2005 documentary *The Wild Parrots of Telegraph Hill*.
- Bus 39 heads to Coit Tower from Fisherman's Wharf – but for scenic walks, take Filbert St or Greenwich St Steps.

Take a Break

Pick up fresh focaccia at Liguria Bakery (p62) to share with parrots (or not) atop Telegraph Hill.

For protein-powered hikes, get Molinari (p62) salami sandwiches.

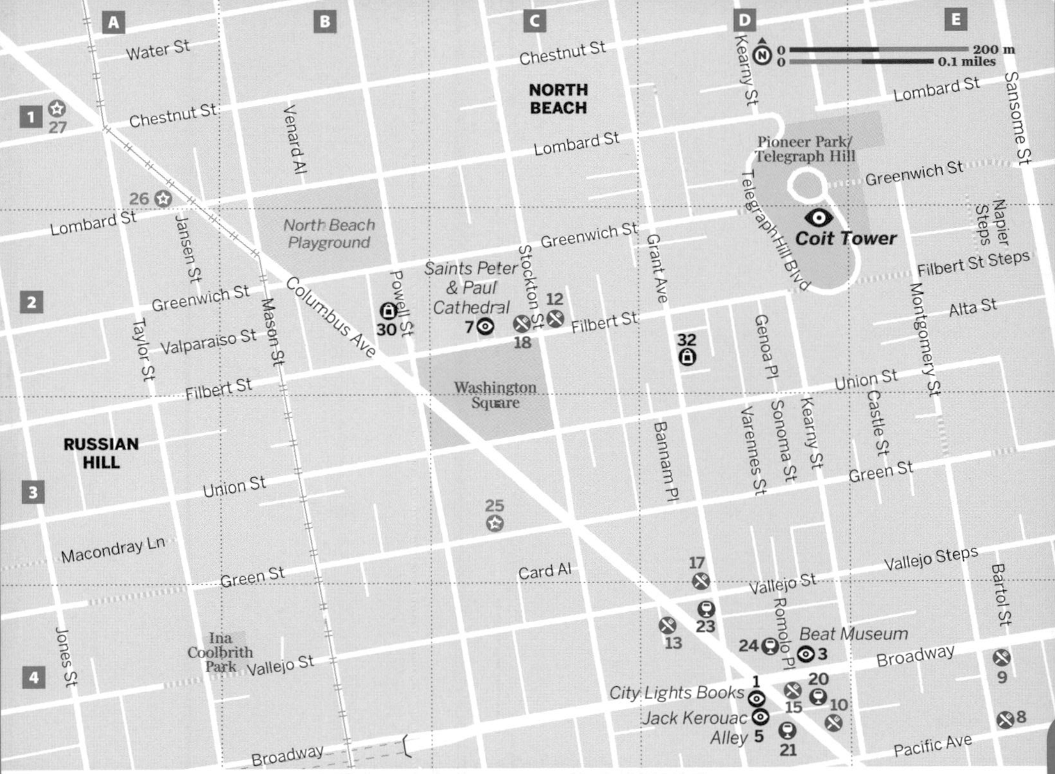
A
B
C
D
E
1
2
3
4
0
200 m
0
0.1 miles
Water St
Chestnut St
NORTH BEACH
Lombard St
Sansome St
Pioneer Park/ Telegraph Hill
Greenwich St
Venard Al
Jansen St
North Beach Playground
Coit Tower
Telegraph Hill Blvd
Napier Steps
Filbert St Steps
Saints Peter & Paul Cathedral
Stockton St
Grant Ave
Columbus Ave
Powell St
Mason St
Taylor St
Valparaiso St
Filbert St
Alta St
Montgomery St
Genoa Pl
Union St
Washington Square
RUSSIAN HILL
Bannam Pl
Varennes St
Sonoma St
Kearny St
Castle St
Green St
Macondray Ln
Card Al
Vallejo Steps
Vallejo St
Bartol St
Romolo Pl
Beat Museum
Broadway
Jones St
Ina Coolbrith Park
City Lights Books
Jack Kerouac Alley
Pacific Ave
1
3
5
7
8
9
10
12
13
15
17
18
20
21
23
24
25
26
27
30
32

Broadway Tunnel
Bernard St
Pacific Ave
Jones St
Taylor St
Auburn St
Mason St
John St
Powell St
Stockton St
Grant Ave
Beckett St
Jackson St
11
19
Kearny St
Columbus Ave
29
Montgomery St
28
22
Chinese Culture Center
4
Jackson St
Stone St
Washington St
Portsmouth Square
Mark Twain St
Tin How Temple
6
Clay St
16
Commercial St
Washington St
Wetmore St
CHINATOWN
14
Waverly Pl
33
31
NOB HILL
2
Chinese Historical Society of America
Sacramento St
Reed St
Priest St
Clay St
Sproule La
Spring St
Pleasant St
Joice St
California St
Sacramento St
Huntington Park
Cushman St
Jones St
Stockton St
Grant Ave
Quincy St
St Mary's Square
Kearny St
California St
Mason St
Powell St
Pine St
Belden Pl
Taylor St
Pine St
Bush St
Claude La
Harlan Pl
Bush St
Sutter St
For reviews see
Top Sights p54
Sights p58
Eating p61
Drinking p64
Entertainment p66
Shopping p68
A
B
C
D
E
5
6
7
8

Chinatown Walks

Local-led, kid-friendly **Chinatown Heritage Walking Tours** (415-986-1822; www.cccsf.us; Chinese Culture Center, Hilton Hotel, 3rd fl, 750 Kearny St; group tour adult $25-30, student $15-20, private tour (1-4 people) $60; tours 10am, noon & 2pm Tue-Sat; ; 1, 8, 10, 12, 30, 41, 45, California, Powell-Mason, Powell-Hyde) guide visitors through the living history of Chinatown in two hours. Themes include The Tale of Two Chinatowns, covering Chinatown's daily life and cultural influence, and From Dynasty to Democracy, which explores Chinatown's role in the US civil rights movement and international human rights struggles. All proceeds support the Chinese Culture Center; bookings can be made online or by phone.

The 41 historic alleyways packed into Chinatown's 22 blocks have seen it all since 1849: Gold Rushes and revolution, incense and opium, fire and icy receptions. **Chinatown Alleyway Tours** (415-984-1478; www.chinatownalleywaytours.org; Portsmouth Sq; adult/student $26/16; tours 11am Sat; ; 1, 8, 10, 12, 30, 41, 45, California, Powell-Mason, Powell-Hyde) offers two-hour Chinatown backstreet walks led by local teens; proceeds support the nonprofit Chinatown Community Development Center.

Sights

City Lights Books CENTER

1 Map p56, D4

Free speech and free spirits have flourished here since 1957, when City Lights founder and poet Lawrence Ferlinghetti and manager Shigeyoshi Murao won a landmark ruling defending their right to publish Allen Ginsberg's magnificent epic poem *Howl*. Celebrate your freedom to read freely in the designated Poet's Chair upstairs overlooking Jack Kerouac Alley, load up on zines on the mezzanine and entertain radical ideas downstairs in the new Pedagogies of Resistance section. (415-362-8193; www.citylights.com; 261 Columbus Ave; 10am-midnight; ; 8, 10, 12, 30, 41, 45, Powell-Mason, Powell-Hyde)

Chinese Historical Society of America MUSEUM

2 Map p56, C6

Picture what it was like to be Chinese in America during the gold rush, transcontinental railroad construction or Beat heyday in this 1932 landmark, built as Chinatown's YWCA by Julia Morgan (chief architect of Hearst Castle). CHSA historians unearth fascinating artifacts, from 1920s silk *qipao* dresses to Chinatown miniatures created by set designer Frank Wong. Exhibits reveal once-popular views of Chinatown, including the sensationalist opium-den exhibit at

Sentinel Building, North Beach

San Francisco's 1915 Panama-Pacific International Expo inviting fairgoers to 'Go Slumming' in Chinatown. (CHSA; 415-391-1188; www.chsa.org; 965 Clay St; adult/student/child $15/10/free; noon-5pm Tue-Fri, 10am-4pm Sat & Sun; ; 1, 8, 30, 45, California, Powell-Mason, Powell-Hyde)

Beat Museum MUSEUM

3 Map p56, D4

The closest you can get to the complete Beat experience without breaking a law. The 1000-plus artifacts in this museum's literary-ephemera collection include the sublime (the banned edition of Ginsberg's *Howl*, with the author's own annotations) and the ridiculous (those Kerouac bobblehead dolls are definite headshakers). Downstairs, watch Beat-era films in ramshackle theater seats redolent with the odors of literary giants, pets and pot. Upstairs, pay your respects at shrines to individual Beat writers. (800-537-6822; www.kerouac.com; 540 Broadway; adult/student $8/5, walking tours $25; museum 10am-7pm, walking tours 2-4pm Sat; 8, 10, 12, 30, 41, 45, Powell-Mason)

Chinese Culture Center GALLERY

4 Map p56, E5

You can see all the way to China from the Hilton's 3rd floor inside this cultural center, which hosts exhibits

ranging from showcases of contemporary Chinese ink-brush painters to installations of kung-fu punching bags studded with fighting words. In odd-numbered years, don't miss the Present Tense Biennial, where 30-plus Bay Area artists present personal takes on Chinese culture. Visit the satellite gallery at 41 Ross Alley solo or on the center's Chinatown Heritage Walking Tours, led by resident Chinatown historians. (415-986-1822; www.cccsf.us; Hilton Hotel, 3rd fl, 750 Kearny St; suggested donation $5; during exhibitions 10am-4pm Tue-Sat; ; 1, 8, 10, 12, 30, 41, 45, California, Powell-Mason, Powell-Hyde)

Jack Kerouac Alley

STREET

5 Map p56, D4

'The air was soft, the stars so fine, the promise of every cobbled alley so great...' This ode by the *On the Road* and *Dharma Bums* author is embedded in his namesake alley, a fittingly poetic, streetwise shortcut between Chinatown and North Beach via the writer's haunts City Lights (p58) and Vesuvio (p65) – Kerouac took literature, Buddhism and beer seriously. (btwn Grant & Columbus Aves; 8, 10, 12, 30, 41, 45, Powell-Mason)

Tin How Temple

TEMPLE

6 Map p56, D6

There was no place to go but up in Chinatown in the 19th century, when laws restricted where Chinese San Franciscans could live and work. Atop barber shops, laundries and diners lining **Waverly Place** (1, 30, California, Powell-Mason), you'll spot lantern-festooned temple balconies. Tin How Temple was built in 1852; its altar miraculously survived the 1906 earthquake. To pay your respects, follow sandalwood-incense aromas up three flights of stairs. Entry is free, but offerings are customary for temple upkeep. No photography inside, please. (Tien Hau Temple; 125 Waverly Pl; donation customary; 10am-4pm, except holidays; 1, 8, 30, 45, California, Powell-Mason, Powell-Hyde)

Saints Peter & Paul Cathedral

CHURCH

7 Map p56, C2

Wedding-cake cravings are inspired by this white, triple-decker 1924 cathedral. The church holds Catholic masses in Italian, Chinese, Latin and English and pulls triple wedding shifts on Saturday – Joe DiMaggio and Marilyn Monroe took wedding photos here, but, since they were both divorced, they weren't permitted to marry in the church (they got hitched at City Hall). The mosaic Dante quote over the entryway echoes Beat poets and Beatles: 'The glory of Him who moves all things/Penetrates and glows throughout the universe.' (415-421-0809; http://salesianssspp.org; 666 Filbert St; 7:30am-12:30pm Mon-Fri, to 5pm Sat & Sun; 8, 30, 39, 41, 45, Powell-Mason)

Understand

The Barbary Coast

By 1854 San Francisco's harbor near Portsmouth Sq was filling with rotting ships abandoned by crews with Gold Rush fever. Here on the ragged piers of the 'Barbary Coast,' a buck might procure whiskey, opium or a woman's company at 500 saloons, 20 theaters and numerous brothels – but buyer beware. Saloon owners like Shanghai Kelly and notorious madam Miss Piggot would ply new arrivals with booze, knock them out with drugs or billy-clubs, and deliver them to sea captains in need of crews. At the gaming tables, luck literally was a lady: women card dealers dealt winning hands to those who engaged their back-room services.

Prohibition and California's 1913 Red Light Abatement Act drove the Barbary Coast's illicit action underground, but it never really went away. US obscenity laws were defied post-WWII in anything-goes North Beach clubs near Broadway and Columbus, where burlesque dancer Carol Doda went topless and comedian Lenny Bruce dropped f-bombs. Today San Francisco is undergoing a Barbary Coast saloon revival, with potent 19th-century-style cocktails served by apparently harmless bartenders – just don't forget to tip.

Eating

Cotogna ITALIAN $$

Chef-owner Michael Tusk racks up James Beard Awards for a quintessentially Italian culinary balancing act: he strikes ideal proportions among a few pristine flavors in rustic pastas, wood-fired pizzas and salt-crusted branzino. Reserve, especially for bargain $55 four-course Sunday suppers with $35 wine pairings – or plan a walk-in late lunch/early dinner. Top-value Italian wine list (most bottles $55). (415-775-8508; www.cotognasf.com; 490 Pacific Ave; mains $19-35; 11:30am-10:30pm Mon-Thu, to 11pm Fri & Sat, 5-9:30pm Sun; ; 10, 12)

Coi CALIFORNIAN $$$

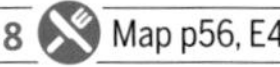

Entire beach vacations are condensed into chef Matthew Kirkley's artful nine-course modern seafood menu. Expect waves of surf, with scant turf – a truffle here, bone marrow there, sunny splashes of California citrus everywhere. Seasonal standouts include Dungeness crab, fluke with caviar, and – nodding to North Beach – mussels morphed into cannoli. Lavish wine pairings ($180); 20% service added. (415-393-9000; www.coirestaurant.com; 373 Broadway; set menu $250; 5:30-10pm Thu-Mon; P; 8, 10, 12, 30, 41, 45, Powell-Mason)

Tosca Cafe

ITALIAN $$

10 Map p56, D4

When this historic North Beach speakeasy was nearly evicted in 2012, devotees like Sean Penn, Robert De Niro and Johnny Depp rallied, and New York star chef April Bloomfield took over. Now the 1930s murals and red-leather banquettes are restored and the revived kitchen serves rustic Italian classics (get the meatballs). Jukebox opera and spiked house cappuccino here deserve SF-landmark status. Reservations essential. (415-986-9651; www.toscacafesf.com; 242 Columbus Ave; mains $15-22; 5pm-2am; 8, 10, 12, 30, 41, 45, Powell-Mason)

Z & Y

CHINESE $$

11 Map p56, D5

Graduate from ho-hum sweet-and-sour and middling *mu-shu* to sensational Szechuan dishes that go down in a blaze of glory. Warm up with spicy pork dumplings and heat-blistered string beans, take on the housemade *tantan* noodles with peanut-chili sauce, and leave lips buzzing with fish poached in flaming chili oil and buried under red Szechuan chili peppers. Go early; worth the inevitable wait. (415-981-8988; www.zandyrestaurant.com; 655 Jackson St; mains $9-20; 11am-9:30pm Sun-Thu, to 11pm Fri & Sat; 8, 10, 12, 30, 45, Powell-Mason, Powell-Hyde)

Liguria Bakery

BAKERY $

12 Map p56, C2

Bleary-eyed art students and Italian grandmothers are in line by 8am for cinnamon-raisin focaccia hot out of the 100-year-old oven, leaving 9am dawdlers a choice of tomato or classic rosemary and garlic, and 11am stragglers out of luck. Take yours in waxed paper or boxed for picnics – but don't kid yourself that you're going to save some for later. Cash only. (415-421-3786; 1700 Stockton St; focaccia $4-6; 8am-1pm Tue-Fri, from 7am Sat; 8, 30, 39, 41, 45, Powell-Mason)

Molinari

DELI $

13 Map p56, D4

Observe quasi-religious North Beach noontime rituals: enter Molinari, and grab a number and a crusty roll. When your number's called, wisecracking staff pile your roll with heavenly fixings: milky buffalo mozzarella, tangy sun-dried tomatoes, translucent sheets of prosciutto di Parma, slabs of legendary house-cured salami, drizzles of olive oil and balsamic. Enjoy hot from the panini press at sidewalk tables. (415-421-2337; www.molinarisalame.com; 373 Columbus Ave; sandwiches $10-13.50; 9am-6pm Mon-Fri, to 5:30pm Sat; 8, 10, 12, 30, 39, 41, 45, Powell-Mason)

Molinari

Mister Jiu's

CHINESE **$$**

14 Map p56, D6

Ever since the gold rush, San Francisco has craved Chinese food, powerful cocktails and hyperlocal specialties – and Mister Jiu's satisfies on all counts. Build your own banquet of Chinese classics with California twists: chanterelle chow mein, Dungeness-crab rice noodles, quail and Mission-fig sticky rice. Cocktail pairings are equally inspired – try jasmine-infused-gin Happiness ($13) with tea-smoked Sonoma-duck confit. (415-857-9688; http://misterjius.com; 28 Waverly Pl; mains $14-45; 5:30-10:30pm Tue-Sat; 30, California)

E' Tutto Qua

ITALIAN **$$**

15 Map p56, D4

The Colosseum is 6000 miles from the corner of Columbus and Broadway, but you'll eat like a gladiator at E' Tutto Qua (translation: It's All Here). Boisterous Roman service and over-the-top decor create a party atmosphere – but they're serious about homemade pasta, grilled meats and top-flight Italian wines. Order the lamb chops and truffled *paccheri* (tube pasta) and emerge victorious. (415-989-1002; www.etuttoqua.com; 270 Columbus Ave; mains $16-30; 5pm-midnight; 8, 10, 12, 30, 41, 45, Powell-Mason)

City View

DIM SUM $

16  Map p56, E6

Take a seat in the sunny dining room and make way for carts loaded with delicate shrimp and leek dumplings, garlicky Chinese broccoli, tangy spare-ribs, coconut-dusted custard tarts and other tantalizing dim sum. Arrive before the midday lunch rush to nab seats in the sunny upstairs room and get first dibs on passing carts. (415-398-2838; http://cityviewdimsum.com; 662 Commercial St; dishes $3-8; 11am-2:30pm Mon-Fri, from 10am Sat & Sun; ; 1, 8, 10, 12, 30, 45, California)

Ristorante Ideale

ITALIAN $$

17  Map p56, D3

Other North Beach restaurants fake Italian accents, but this trattoria has Italians in the kitchen, on the floor and at the table. Roman chef-owner Maurizio Bruschi serves authentic, al dente *bucatini amatriciana* (tube pasta with tomato-pecorino sauce and house-cured pancetta) and ravioli and gnocchi handmade in-house ('of course!'). North Beach's best-value Italian wine list ensures everyone goes home with Italian accents. (415-391-4129; www.idealerestaurant.com; 1309 Grant Ave; pasta $16-22; 5:30-10:30pm Mon-Thu, to 11pm Fri & Sat, 5-10pm Sun; 8, 10, 12, 30, 41, 45, Powell-Mason)

Mama's

BRUNCH $

18 Map p56, C2

Generations of North Beachers have entrusted the most important meal of the day to Mama and Papa Sanchez, whose sunny Victorian storefront diner has soothed barbaric Barbary Coast hangovers for 50 years. Local farm-egg omelets and *kugelhopf* (house-baked brioche) French toast are cure-alls, but weekend specials like Dungeness-crab eggs Benedict make waits down the block worthwhile. Cash only. (415-362-6421; www.mamas-sf.com; 1701 Stockton St; brunch mains $10-14; 8am-3pm Tue-Sun; ; 8, 30, 39, 41, 45, Powell-Mason)

Drinking

Comstock Saloon

BAR

19  Map p56, D5

Relieving yourself in the marble trough below the bar is no longer advisable – Emperor Norton is watching from above – but otherwise this 1907 Victorian saloon brings back the Barbary Coast's glory days with authentic pisco punch and martini-precursor Martinez (gin, vermouth, bitters, maraschino liqueur). Reserve booths or back-parlor seating to hear on nights when ragtime-jazz bands play. (415-617-0071; www.comstocksaloon.com; 155 Columbus Ave; 4pm-midnight Sun-Mon, to 2am Tue-Thu & Sat, noon-2am Fri; 8, 10, 12, 30, 45, Powell-Mason)

Specs

BAR

20 Map p56, D4

The walls here are plastered with merchant-marine memorabilia, and you'll be plastered too if you try to keep up with the salty characters

holding court in back. Surrounded by seafaring mementos – including walrus genitalia over the bar – your order seems obvious: pitcher of Anchor Steam, coming right up. Cash only. (Specs Twelve Adler Museum Cafe; ☎415-421-4112; 12 William Saroyan Pl; ⏲5pm-2am; 🚌8, 10, 12, 30, 41, 45, 🚋Powell-Mason)

Vesuvio

BAR

21 Map p56, D4

Guy walks into a bar, roars and leaves. Without missing a beat, the bartender says to the next customer, 'Welcome to Vesuvio, honey – what can I get you?' Jack Kerouac blew off Henry Miller to go on a bender here and, after you've joined neighborhood characters on the stained-glass mezzanine for microbrews or Kerouacs (rum, tequila and OJ), you'll see why. (☎415-362-3370; www.vesuvio.com; 255 Columbus Ave; ⏲8am-2am; 🚌8, 10, 12, 30, 41, 45, 🚋Powell-Mason)

Li Po

BAR

22 Map p56, D5

Beat a hasty retreat to red-vinyl booths where Allen Ginsberg and Jack Kerouac debated the meaning of life under a golden Buddha. Enter the 1937 faux-grotto doorway and dodge red lanterns to place your order: Tsingtao beer or a sweet, sneaky-strong Chinese mai tai made with *baijiu* (rice liquor). Brusque bartenders, basement bathrooms, cash only – a world-class dive bar. (☎415-982-0072; www.lipolounge.com; 916 Grant Ave; ⏲2pm-2am; 🚌8, 30, 45, 🚋Powell-Mason, Powell-Hyde)

Caffe Trieste

CAFE

23 Map p56, D4

Poetry on bathroom walls, opera on the jukebox, live accordion jams and sightings of Beat poet-laureate Lawrence Ferlinghetti: this is North Beach at its best, since the 1950s. Linger over legendary espresso and scribble your screenplay under the Sardinian fishing mural just as young Francis Ford Coppola did. Perhaps you've heard of the movie: *The Godfather*. Cash only. (☎415-392-6739; www.caffetrieste.com; 601 Vallejo St; ⏲6:30am-10pm Sun-Thu, to 11pm Fri & Sat; 📶; 🚌8, 10, 12, 30, 41, 45)

Local Life

Red Blossom Tea Company

Several Grant Ave tea importers offer free samples, but the hard sell may begin before you finish sipping. For more relaxed, enlightening tea tasting, **Red Blossom Tea Company** (Map p56, D6; ☎415-395-0868; www.redblossomtea.com; 831 Grant Ave; ⏲10am-6:30pm Mon-Sat, to 6pm Sun; 🚌1, 10, 12, 30, 35, 41, 🚋Powell-Mason, Powell-Hyde, California) offers half-hour courses with four to five tastings and preparation tips to maximize flavor ($30 for up to four participants; drop-in weekdays, reserve ahead weekends).

15 Romolo BAR

24  Map p56, D4

Strap on your spurs: it's gonna be a wild Western night at this back-alley Basque saloon squeezed between burlesque joints. The strong survive the Suckerpunch (bourbon, sherry, hibiscus, lemon, Basque bitters), but the Basque Firing Squad (mezcal, Basque Patxaran liqueur, grenadine, lime, bitters) ends the night with a bang. Bask in $20 sangria pitchers at the 5:30pm-to-7pm happy hours. (415-398-1359; www.15romolo.com; 15 Romolo Pl; 5pm-2am Mon-Fri, from 11:30am Sat & Sun; 8, 10, 12, 30, 41, 45, Powell-Mason)

Top Tip

Parking Luck

You'd be lucky to find parking anywhere near Chinatown or North Beach, but a free space in the **Good Luck Parking Garage** (Map p56, C4; www.sfmta.com/getting-around/parking/parking-garages/north-beach-garage; 735 Vallejo St; parking per hour $3.50; 10, 12, 30, 41, 45, Powell-Mason) brings double happiness. Each parking spot offers fortune-cookie wisdom stenciled onto the asphalt: 'You have already found your true love. Stop looking.' These car-locating omens are brought to you by West Coast artists Harrell Fletcher and Jon Rubin, who also gathered the photographs of local residents' Chinese and Italian ancestors that grace the entry in heraldic emblems.

Devil's Acre BAR

Magic potions and quack cures are proudly served by this apothecary-style Barbary Coast saloon (see 15 Map p56, D4). Tartly quaffable Lachlan's Antiscorbutic (lime, sea salt, two kinds of gin) is a surefire cure for scurvy and/or sobriety; if you're feeling flush, get the Prospector (pisco, armagnac, Gold Rush bitters). There's happy hour until 7pm, but no food – take your medicine. (415-766-4363; www.thedevilsacre.com; 256 Columbus Ave; 5pm-2am Tue, from 3pm Wed-Sat, 5pm-midnight Sun & Mon; 8, 10, 12, 30, 41, 45, Powell-Mason)

Entertainment

Beach Blanket Babylon CABARET

25 Map p56, C3

Snow White searches for Prince Charming in San Francisco: what could possibly go wrong? The Disney-spoof musical-comedy cabaret has been running since 1974, but topical jokes keep it outrageous and wigs big as parade floats are gasp-worthy. Spectators must be over 21 to handle racy humor, except at cleverly sanitized Sunday matinees. Reservations essential; arrive one hour early for best seats. (BBB; 415-421-4222; www.beachblanketbabylon.com; 678 Green St; $25-130; shows 8pm Wed, Thu & Fri, 6pm & 9pm Sat, 2pm & 5pm Sun; 8, 30, 39, 41, 45, Powell-Mason)

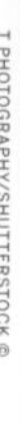

Dim sum at a Chinese restaurant in San Francisco

Cobb's Comedy Club

COMEDY

26 Map p56, A1

There's no room to be shy at Cobb's, where bumper-to-bumper shared tables make the audience cozy – and vulnerable. The venue is known for launching local talent and giving big-name acts (Louis CK, John Oliver, Ali Wong) a place to try risky new material. Check the website for shows and showcases like Really Funny Comedians (Who Happen to Be Women). Two-drink minimum. (415-928-4320; www.cobbscomedyclub.com; 915 Columbus Ave; $13-45; 8, 30, 39, 41, 45, Powell-Mason)

Bimbo's 365 Club

LIVE MUSIC

27 Map p56, A1

Get your kicks at this 1931 speakeasy with stiff drinks, bawdy vintage bar murals, parquet dance floors for high-stepping like Rita Hayworth (she was in the chorus line here) and intimate live shows by the likes of Beck, Pinback, Guided by Voices and Nouvelle Vague. Dress snazzy and bring cash to tip the ladies'-powder-room attendant. Two-drink minimum; cash only. (415-474-0365; www.bimbos365club.com; 1025 Columbus Ave; from $20; box office 10am-4pm; 8, 30, 39, 41, 45, Powell-Mason)

Shopping

Golden Gate Fortune Cookie Company

FOOD & DRINKS

28 Map p56, D5

Make a fortune at this bakery, where cookies are stamped from vintage presses – just as they were in 1909, when fortune cookies were invented for SF's Japanese Tea Garden (p143). Write your own fortunes for custom cookies (50¢ each), or get cookies with regular or risqué fortunes (pro tip: add 'in bed' to regular ones). Cash only; 50¢ tip for photos. (415-781-3956; 56 Ross Alley; 9am-6pm; 8, 30, 45, Powell-Mason, Powell-Hyde)

Eden & Eden

GIFTS & SOUVENIRS

29 Map p56, E5

Detour from reality at Eden & Eden, a Dadaist design boutique where bats with outstretched wings serve as necklaces, galaxies twinkle on dresses, shaggy tea cozies make teapots look bearded, and those suede lips are coin purses that swallow loose change. Prices are surprisingly reasonable for far-out, limited-edition and repurposed-vintage finds from local and international designers. (415-983-0490; www.edenandeden.com; 560 Jackson St; 10am-7pm Mon-Fri, to 6pm Sat; 8, 10, 12, 41)

San Francisco Rock Posters & Collectibles

ANTIQUES

30 Map p56, B2

Are you ready to rock? Enter this trippy temple to classic rock gods – but leave your lighters at home, because these concert posters are valuable. Expect to pay hundreds for first-run psychedelic Fillmore concert posters featuring the Grateful Dead – but you can score bargain handbills for San Francisco acts like Santana, the Dead Kennedys and Sly and the Family Stone. (415-956-6749; www.rockposters.com; 1851 Powell St; 10am-6pm Mon-Sat; 8, 30, 39, 41, 45, Powell-Mason)

Chinatown Kite Shop

GIFTS & SOUVENIRS

31 Map p56, D6

Be the star of Crissy Field and wow any kids in your life with a fierce 9ft-long flying dragon, a pirate-worthy wild parrot (SF's city bird), surreal floating legs or a flying panda that looks understandably stunned. Pick up a two-person, papier-mâché lion-dance costume and invite a date to bust ferocious moves with you next lunar new year. (415-989-5182; www.chinatownkite.com; 717 Grant Ave; 10am-8pm; ; 1, 10, 12, 30, 35, 41, Powell-Hyde, Powell-Mason, California)

EMMA WISHNOW/SHUTTERSTOCK ©

Fortune cookies

Aria

ANTIQUES

32 Map p56, D2

Find inspiration for your own North Beach epic poem on Aria's weathered wood counters, piled with anatomical drawings of starfish, castle keys lost in gutters a century ago, rusty numbers pried from French village walls and 19th-century letters still in their wax-sealed envelopes. Hours are erratic whenever owner and chief scavenger Bill Haskell is treasure-hunting abroad, so call ahead. (415-433-0219; 1522 Grant Ave; 11am-6pm Mon-Sat; 8, 30, 39, 41, 45, Powell-Mason)

Far East Flea Market

GIFTS & SOUVENIRS

33 Map p56, D6

The shopping equivalent of crack, this bottomless store is dangerously cheap and certain to make you giddy and delusional. Of course you can get that 2ft-long samurai sword through airport security! There's no such thing as too many action figures, emoji pillows or paper lanterns! Step away from the $1 Golden Gate Bridge snow globes while there's still time... (415-989-8588; 729 Grant Ave; 10am-9:30pm; 1, 10, 12, 30, 35, 41, Powell-Mason, Powell-Hyde, California)

Local Life
Russian Hill & Nob Hill Secrets

Getting There

Nob Hill stands between downtown and Chinatown; Russian Hill abuts Fisherman's Wharf and North Beach.

🚋 **Cable car** California St, Powell-Hyde and Powell-Mason cable cars cover steep hillside streets.

Cloud nine can't compare to the upper reaches of Nob Hill and Russian Hill, where hilltop gardens, literary landmarks and divine views await discovery up flower-lined stairway walks. If the climb and the sights don't leave you completely weak in the knees, try staggering back downhill after a couple of Nob Hill cocktails. Now you understand why San Francisco invented cable cars.

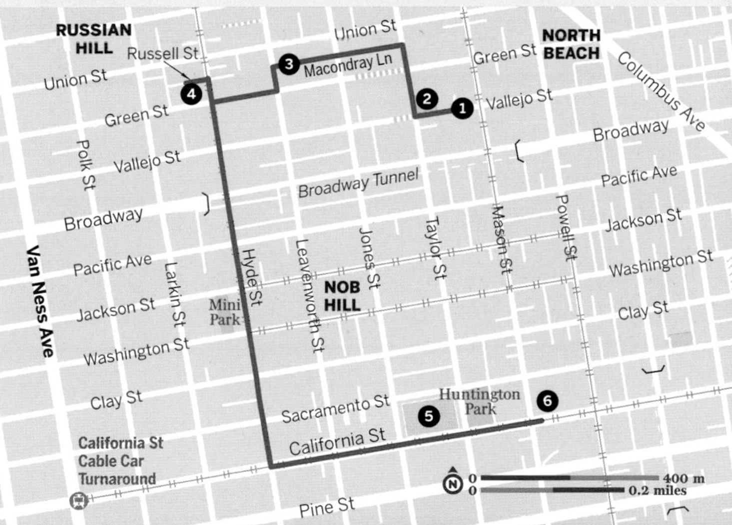

❶ Conquer Vallejo Street Steps

Begin your ascent of Russian Hill from North Beach, where **Vallejo Street Steps** (Vallejo St, btwn Mason & Jones Sts; Powell-Mason, Powell-Hyde) rise toward Jones St past Zen gardens and flower-framed apartments. When fog blows, listen for whooshing in the treetops and the irregular music of wind chimes. Stop to catch your breath, then turn around and lose it again with seagull's-eye views of the Bay Bridge.

❷ Wax Poetic at Ina Coolbrith Park

On San Francisco's literary scene, all roads eventually lead to Ina Coolbrith, California's first poet laureate; colleague of Mark Twain and Ansel Adams; and mentor to Jack London, Isadora Duncan, George Sterling and Charlotte Perkins Gilman. One association she kept secret: her uncle was Mormon prophet Joseph Smith. **Ina Coolbrith Park** (cnr Vallejo & Taylor Sts; 10, 12, Powell-Mason) is a fitting honor: secret and romantic, with exclamation-inspiring vistas.

❸ Discover Mysterious Macondray Lane

The scenic route down from Ina Coolbrith Park – via steep stairs, past gravity-defying wooden cottages – is so charming, it could be a scene from a novel. And so it is: Armistead Maupin used **Macondray Lane** (btwn Jones & Leavenworth Sts; 41, 45, Powell-Mason, Powell-Hyde) as the model for Barbary Lane in his *Tales of the City* mysteries.

❹ Spot Kerouac's Love Shack

This **modest house** (29 Russell St; 41, 45, Powell-Hyde) on a quiet alley witnessed major drama in 1951–52, when Jack Kerouac shacked up with Neal and Carolyn Cassady to pound out his 120ft-long scroll draft of *On the Road*. Jack and Carolyn became lovers at Neal's suggestion, but Carolyn frequently kicked them both out. Neal was allowed back for the birth of John Allen Cassady (named for Jack and Allen Ginsberg).

❺ Find Unexpected Graces at Grace Cathedral

Hop the Powell-Hyde cable car to Nob Hill's crest, graced by Gothic **Grace Cathedral** (415-749-6300; www.gracecathedral.org; 1100 California St; suggested donation adult/child $3/2, services free; 8am-6pm Mon-Sat, to 7pm Sun, services 8:30am, 11am & 6pm Sun; 1, California). Labyrinths outside and indoors set a contemplative mood, while stained-glass windows celebrate religious dissidents and scientists. Grace's commitment to social issues is embodied in Keith Haring's cartoon-angel altarpiece for AIDS Memorial Chapel.

❻ Drink up a Storm at the Tonga Room

Tonight's weather: partly foggy, with 100% chance of tropical rainstorms every 20 minutes inside the **Tonga Room** (415-772-5278 reservations; www.tongaroom.com; Fairmont San Francisco, 950 Mason St; cover $5-7; 5-11:30pm Sun, Wed & Thu, to 12:30am Fri & Sat; 1, California, Powell-Mason, Powell-Hyde). Don't worry, you'll stay dry in your grass hut – the rain only falls on the indoor pool, where cover bands play on an island after 8pm.

Explore

Downtown & SoMa

Get to know SF from the inside out, from art museums to farmers markets. Discover fine dining that's unfussy yet fabulous, and find out why some cocktails are worth double digits – and sleep is overrated. Social-media headquarters rub shoulders with drag venues South of Market St (SoMa), and after 10pm, everyone gets down and dirty on the dance floor.

The Sights in a Day

Graze your way through the **Ferry Building** (p74) and its year-round, thrice-weekly farmers market to a fortifying bayside brunch at **Boulette's Larder** (p75). Now you're ready for your SoMa art binge: check out the **San Francisco Museum of Modern Art** (p80) and its impressive new galleries, and save time for a visit to the **Contemporary Jewish Museum** (p84), **California Historical Society** (p84) or **Museum of the African Diaspora** (p84).

Hop the Powell-Hyde **cable car** (p76) to giddy Golden Gate Bridge views. Return downtown for the happy hour of your choice: oysters and bubbly at **Hog Island Oyster Company** (p75), Prohibition-pedigreed cocktails at **Bar Agricole** (p88), pints at **Irish Bank** (p89) or knockout Pisco Punch at **Rickhouse** (p88).

Plan the rest of your night around a SoMa club crawl, **ACT** (p90) theater tickets, reservations at **Benu** (p86), or a drag extravaganzas at **Oasis** (p90).

Top Sights

Ferry Building (p74)

Cable Cars (p76)

San Francisco Museum of Modern Art (p80)

Best of San Francisco

Eating Out

Benu (p86)

Museums

Contemporary Jewish Museum (p84)

California Historical Society (p84)

LGBT

EndUp (p89)

Oasis (p90)

Getting There

Ⓜ **Streetcars** and Bay Area rapid Transport (BART) subways run along Market St.

Bus East–west buses include 14 Mission and 47 Harrison (to Fisherman's Wharf); north–south include 27 Bryant (Mission to Russian Hill) and 19 Polk.

Car Garage at Mission and 5th Sts.

Top Sights
Ferry Building

Other towns have gourmet ghettos, but San Francisco puts its love of food front and center at the Ferry Building. The once-grand port was overshadowed by a 1950s elevated freeway – until the overpass collapsed in 1989's Loma Prieta earthquake. The Ferry Building survived and became a symbol of San Francisco's reinvention, marking your arrival onto America's forward-thinking food frontier.

Map p82, H2

415-983-8030

www.ferrybuildingmarketplace.com

cnr Market St & the Embarcadero

10am-7pm Mon-Fri, 8am-6pm Sat, 11am-5pm Sun

2, 6, 9, 14, 21, 31, M Embarcadero, B Embarcadero

Ferry Building

Hog Island Oyster Company

Decadence with a conscience: sustainably farmed, local oysters are served raw and cooked with Sonoma bubbly at **Hog Island** (☎415-391-7117; www.hogislandoysters.com; 4 oysters $14; ⏲11am-9pm). Oysters are half-price and pints $4 from 5pm to 7pm Monday to Thursday.

Boulette's Larder

Dinner theater doesn't get better than brunch at **Boulette's** (☎415-399-1155; www.bouletteslarder.com; ⏲Larder 8-10:30am & 11:30am-3pm Tue-Sat, 10am-2:30pm Sun, Boulibar 11:30am-9:30pm Tue-Fri, to 8pm Sat) communal table, in a working kitchen amid a swirl of chefs and with views of the Bay Bridge.

Slanted Door

Taste the California dream at **Slanted Door** (☎415-861-8032; www.slanteddoor.com; mains $18-42; ⏲11am-4:30pm & 5:30-10pm Mon-Sat, 11:30am-10pm Sun), where James Beard Award–winning chef-owner Charles Phan serves California-fresh, Vietnamese-inspired dishes with bay views. Book ahead, or picnic on takeout.

Mijita

Sustainable fish tacos reign supreme and agua fresca (fruit punch) is made with fresh juice at James Beard Award–winning chef-owner Traci Des Jardins' casual **Mijita** (☎415-399-0814; www.mijitasf.com; dishes $4-10; ⏲10am-7pm Mon-Thu, to 8pm Fri, 9am-8pm Sat, 9am-3pm Sun;), paying tribute to her Mexican grandmother's cooking.

☑ Top Tips

- Among the locavore gourmet stalls lining the grand arrivals hall, don't miss dessert at Recchiuti Chocolates.
- For bayside picnics, find benches flanking the bronze statue of Gandhi by the ferry docks, or head to Pier 14 for perches with bay views.
- Across the Embarcadero from the Ferry Building in Justin Herman Plaza, lunchtime picnickers mingle with wild parrots, protestors, skaters and craftspeople.

✕ Take a Break

During the Tuesday, Thursday and Saturday **farmers markets** (☎415-291-3276; www.cuesa.org; street food $3-12; cnr Market St & the Embarcadero; ⏲10am-2pm Tue & Thu, from 8am Sat;), hit gourmet food stalls flanking the Ferry Building's southwestern corner.

Top Sights
Cable Cars

Roller-coaster rides can't compare to the death-defying thrills of riding a 15,000lb cable car down San Francisco hills, careening toward oncoming traffic. But Andrew Hallidie's 1873 contraptions have held up miraculously well on these giddy slopes, and groaning brakes and clanging brass bells add to the carnival-ride thrills. Powell-Mason cars are quickest to reach Fisherman's Wharf; Powell-Hyde cars are more scenic; and the original east–west California St line is the least crowded.

Map p82, D2

www.sfmta.com

cnr Powell & Market Sts

Powell-Mason, Mason-Hyde M Powell, B Powell

Powell-Hyde cable car

Powell-Hyde Cable Car

The ascent up Nob Hill feels like the world's longest roller-coaster climb – but on the Powell-Hyde cable car, the biggest thrills are still ahead. This cable car bobs up and down hills, with the Golden Gate Bridge popping in and out of view on Russian Hill. Hop off the cable car at Lombard St to walk the zigzagging route to North Beach. Otherwise, stop and smell the roses along stairway walks to shady Macondray Lane (p71) and blooming Ina Coolbrith Park (p71).

Powell-Mason Cable Car

The Powell-Hyde line may have multi-million-dollar vistas, but the Powell-Mason line has more culture. Detour atop Nob Hill for tropical cocktails and indoor typhoons at the vintage tiki Tonga Room (p71), then resume the ride to Chinatown. The route cuts through North Beach at **Washington Sq** (http://sfrecpark.org/destination/washington-square; cnr Columbus Ave & Union St; 8, 30, 39, 41, 45, Powell-Mason), where you're surrounded by pizza possibilities and alleyways named after Beat poets. The terminus at Bay and Taylor Sts is handy for visiting two truly riveting attractions: the USS Pampanito (p37) and the Musée Mécanique (p37).

California Street Cable Car

History buffs and crowd-shy visitors prefer San Francisco's oldest cable-car line: the California St cable car, in operation since 1878. This divine ride west heads through Chinatown past **Old St Mary's Cathedral** (415-288-3800; www.oldsaintmarys.org; 660 California St; cathedral 11am-6pm Mon & Tue, to 7pm Wed-Fri, 9am-6:30pm Sat, to 4:30pm Sun; 1, 30, 45, California) and climbs Nob Hill to Grace Cathedral (p71). Hop off

☑ Top Tips

- Cable car lines operate 6am to 1am daily; for schedules, see http://transit.511.org.
- One-way tickets cost $7, with no on-and-off privileges. If you're planning to stop en route, get a Muni Passport (per day $21).
- This 19th-century transport vehicle isn't childproof – you won't find car seats or seat belts.
- Cable cars are not accessible for people with disabilities.
- Cable cars make rolling stops. To board on hills, act fast: leap onto the baseboard and grab the closest hand-strap.

Take a Break

Hop off for cocktails and indoor monsoons at the **Tonga Room** (p71).

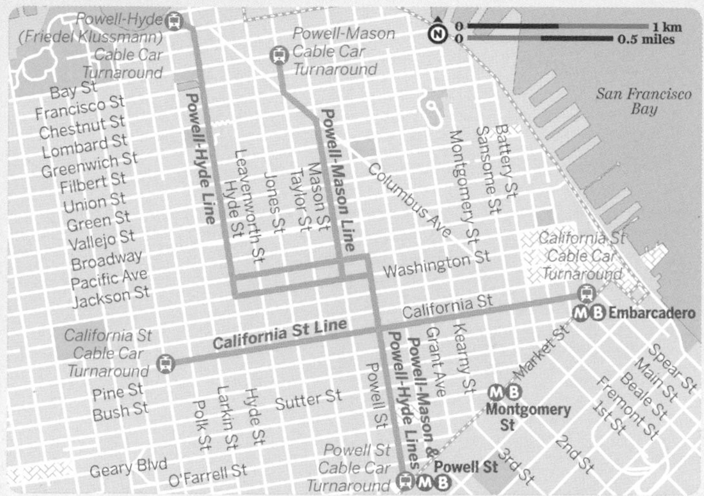

at Polk St for **Swan Oyster Depot** (415-673-1101; 1517 Polk St; dishes $10-25; 10:30am-5:30pm Mon-Sat; 1, 19, 47, 49, California), tempting boutiques and cocktail bars. The Van Ness Ave terminus is a few blocks northeast of Japantown.

Powell Street Cable-Car Turnaround

At Powell and Market Sts, operators slooowly turn Powell-Hyde and Powell-Mason cable cars around on a revolving wooden platform. Tourists line up here to secure a seat, with street performers and doomsday preachers for entertainment. Locals hop on further uphill.

Friedel Klussmann Cable-Car Turnaround

The Powell-Hyde turnaround at Fisherman's Wharf is named after the gardener who rallied her ladies' garden club in 1947 against the mayor's scheme to replace Powell cable cars with buses. In a public vote, the mayor lost to 'The Cable Car Lady' by a landslide. Upon her death in 1986, cable cars citywide were draped in black.

Cable Car Museum

Hear that whirring beneath the cable-car tracks? That's the sound of the cables that pull the cars, and they all connect inside the city's cable-car

Understand

The Cable Car's Timeless Technology

Legend has it that the idea of cable cars occurred to Hallidie in 1869, after he watched a horse carriage struggle up Jackson St – and witnessed a terrible crash when one horse slipped on wet cobblestones and the carriage tumbled downhill. Such accidents were considered inevitable on steep San Francisco hills, but Hallidie knew better. His father was the Scottish inventor of wire cable, used to haul ore out of mines during the gold rush. If hemp-and-metal cable was strong enough to haul rocks through High Sierra snowstorms, surely it could transport San Franciscans through fog.

'Wire-rope railway' was a name that didn't inspire confidence, and skeptical city planners granted the inventor just three months to make his contraption operational by August 1, 1873. Hallidie missed his city deadline by four hours when his cable car was poised on Jones St, ready for the descent. The cable-car operator was terrified, and the story goes that Hallidie himself grabbed the brake and steered the car downhill.

By the 1890s, 53 miles of track crisscrossed the city. Hallidie became a rich man, and he even ran for mayor. But despite his civic contributions and US citizenship, he was defamed as an opportunistic Englishman and lost the race. He remained a lifelong inventor, earning 300 patents and becoming a prominent member of the California Academy of Sciences.

barn. Grips, engines, braking mechanisms...if these warm your gearhead heart, take the California line to the **Cable Car Museum** (415-474-1887; www.cablecarmuseum.org; 1201 Mason St; donations appreciated; 10am-6pm Apr-Sep, to 5pm Oct-Mar; ; Powell-Mason, Powell-Hyde) in Nob Hill. See three original 1870s cable cars and watch cables whir over massive bull wheels – as awesome a feat of physics as it was in 1873.

Top Sights
San Francisco Museum of Modern Art

The expanded SFMOMA is a mind-boggling feat, tripled in size to accommodate a sprawling collection of modern masterworks and 19 concurrent exhibitions over 10 floors – but, then again, SFMOMA has defied limits ever since its 1935 founding. SFMOMA was a visionary early investor in then-emerging art forms including photography, installations, video, performance art, digital art and industrial design.

Map p82, E3

415-357-4000

www.sfmoma.org

adult/under 18yr/student $25/free/$19

10am-5pm Fri-Tue, to 9pm Thu, public spaces from 9am

5, 6, 7, 14, 19, 21, 31, 38, M Montgomery, B Montgomery

German Art after 1960: The Fisher Collection exhibition at SFMOMA

Expanding Collections

After a dramatic 2016 expansion, the SFMOMA now offers free access to ground-floor galleries and a dramatic entrance via Richard Serra's mammoth rusted-steel maze. The unprecedented donation of over 1100 major modern works by the Fisher family (founders of SF-based clothiers Gap, Old Navy and Banana Republic) was the catalyst behind the half-billion-dollar extension, which has added new galleries around Mario Botta's original periscope-shaped atrium.

Suggested Itinerary

Start on the 3rd floor with SFMOMA's standout **photography** collection, featuring great postwar Japanese photographers Shomei Tomatsu and Daido Moriyama alongside pioneering West Coast photographers like Ansel Adams and Dorothea Lange. Meditate amid sunwashed, tone-on-tone paintings in the Agnes Martin room surrounded by 4th floor **Minimalists**, then get an eyeful of Warhol's silver Elvis in **Pop Art** on the 5th floor.

The 6th floor hosts poignant **video art** by Shirin Neshat and William Kentridge, while the top floor reaches peak art freak with **experimental works**. Head down via the atrium to see how SFMOMA began, with colorful local characters admiring equally colorful characters by Diego Rivera, Frida Kahlo and Henri Matisse.

Museum Store

Start your own collection of SFMOMA design objects, statement jewelry and stylish housewares at the ground-floor Museum Store. In the well-stocked book section, you can pick up catalogs from recent exhibits, coffee-table books, cookbooks and even artsy tomes for tots.

☑ Top Tips

- ▶ For weekend visits and special exhibits, book tickets ahead online.
- ▶ Visitors under age 18 enjoy free admission, but they must have a ticket for entry.
- ▶ The museum offers 45,000ft of public space that you can explore without a ticket.
- ▶ Reserve weeks/months ahead to dine at SFMOMA's acclaimed gallery of world cuisine **In Situ** (☎415-941-6050; http://insitu.sfmoma.org; SFMOMA, 151 3rd St; mains $14-34; ⊙11am-3:30pm Mon & Tue, 11am-3:30pm & 5-9pm Thu-Sun; 🚌14, B Montgomery, M Montgomery).

✕ Take a Break

Sunny days are ideal for restorative coffee and impromptu panini in the **rooftop cafe and sculpture garden**.

A
B
C
D
1
2
3
4
5
0 400 m
0 0.2 miles
McAllister St
Van Ness Ave
Grove St
Hayes St
Fell St
Elm St
Polk St
Larkin St
Hyde St
Ellis St
Turk St
Golden Gate Ave
Leavenworth St
Geary St
O'Farrell St
Jones St
Taylor St
Eddy St
Mason St
Dr Carlton B Goodlett Pl
Larkin St
McAllister St
Civic Center Plaza
United Nations Plaza
San Francisco Main Library
Powell St Cable Car Turnaround
Bank of America
Market St
Civic Center
Powell St Cable Car Turnaround
Powell St
Stevenson St
Jessie St
Jessie St
Mission St
Minna St
Natoma St
Howard St
Tehama St
Tehama St
Clementina St
SOUTH OF MARKET (SOMA)
Folsom St
Shipley St
Clara St
Harrison St
James Lick Skwy
Autoreturn
Bryant St
Brannan St
Bluxome St
Townsend St
11th St
10th St
Grace St
9th St
8th St
7th St
6th St
Mary St
5th St
Dore Al
Langton St
Moss St
Russ St
Harriet St
Morris St
Gilbert St
Harriet St
Victoria Manalo Draves Park
22
27
23
24
14
26
19
17
18
32
21
25
For reviews see
Top Sights p74
Sights p84
Eating p86
Drinking p88
Entertainment p90
Shopping p92

E
F
G
H
1
2
3
4
5
CHINATOWN
UNION SQUARE
FINANCIAL DISTRICT (FIDI)
Powell St
California St
Pine St
Grant Ave
Bush St
Stockton St
Sutter St
Post St
Maiden La
Kearny St
Montgomery St
Sacramento St
Columbus Ave
Pacific Ave
Jackson St
Washington St
Sansome St
Battery St
Front St
Davis St
The Embarcadero
Walton Park
Maritime Plaza
Whaleship Plaza
Embarcadero Center
Justin Herman Plaza
Ferry Building
Union Square
American Automobile Association
49 Geary
Market St
Montgomery St
Embarcadero
California St Cable Car Turnaround
Yerba Buena La
Stevenson St
Contemporary Jewish Museum
California Historical Society
Mission St
Audiffred Building
Pier 2
Minna St
San Francisco Museum of Modern Art
Museum of the African Diaspora
Howard St
1st St
Fremont St
Beale St
Main St
Spear St
Steuart St
Children's Creativity Museum
New Montgomery St
Folsom St
Folsom St
4th St
Bonifacio St
Rizal St
3rd St
Hawthorne St
2nd St
Pier 22½
Harrison St
Pier 24
James Lick Skwy
Bay Bridge
Embarcadero South St
Pier 26
Bryant St
Taber Pl
South Park
Zoe St
Ritch St
Delancey St
Pier 28
Pier 30
Pier 32
Brannan St
Stanford St
Pier 34
Pier 36
San Francisco Bay
1
2
3
4
5
6
7
8
9
10
11
12
13
15
16
20
28
29
30
31

Sights

Contemporary Jewish Museum

MUSEUM

2 Map p82, E3

That upended blue-steel box miraculously balancing on one corner isn't sculpture but the Yerba Buena Lane entry to the Contemporary Jewish Museum – an institution that upends conventional ideas about art and religion. Exhibits here are compelling explorations of Jewish ideals and visionaries, including writer Gertrude Stein, rock promoter Bill Graham, cartoonist Roz Chast and filmmaker Stanley Kubrick. (415-344-8800; www.thecjm.org; 736 Mission St; adult/student/child $14/12/free; after 5pm Thu $5; 11am-5pm Mon, Tue & Fri-Sun, to 8pm Thu; ; 14, 30, 45, B Montgomery, M Montgomery)

Top Tip

Emperor Norton's Fantastic Time Machine

Huzzah, San Francisco has invented time-travel contraptions! They're called shoes, and you wear them to follow the self-appointed Emperor Norton (aka historian Joseph Amster) on a quirky walking tour through San Francisco history. **Emperor Norton's Fantastic Time Machine** (415-644-8513; www.emperornortontour.com; $20; 11am & 2:30pm Thu & Sat, 11am Sun; 30, 38, B Powell St, M Powell St, Powell-Mason, Powell-Hyde) leads you across 2 miles of the most dastardly, scheming, uplifting and urban-legendary terrain on Earth...or at least west of Berkeley.

Museum of the African Diaspora

MUSEUM

3 Map p82, E3

MoAD assembles an international cast of characters to tell the epic story of diaspora, including a moving video of slave narratives told by Maya Angelou. Standouts among quarterly changing exhibits have included homages to '80s New Wave icon Grace Jones, architect David Adjaye's photographs of contemporary African landmarks and Alison Saar's sculptures of figures marked by history. Public events include poetry slams, Yoruba spiritual music celebrations and lectures examining the legacy of the Black Panthers' free-school-breakfast program. (MoAD; 415-358-7200; www.moadsf.org; 685 Mission St; adult/child/student $10/free/$5; 11am-6pm Wed-Sat, noon-5pm Sun; P ; 14, 30, 45, M Montgomery, B Montgomery)

California Historical Society

MUSEUM

4 Map p82, E3

Enter a Golden State of enlightenment at this Californiana treasure trove, featuring themed exhibitions drawn from the museum's million-plus California photographs, paintings and ephemera. Recent exhibits have unearthed

Prohibition-era wine labels, protest posters from the Summer of Love and 1971 instructions for interpretive-dancing your way through San Francisco by dance pioneer Anna Halprin. Events are rare opportunities to discuss 1970s underground comix, 1940s SF gay bars and gold rush–era saloon menu staples (whiskey, opium and tamales). (415-357-1848; www.californiahistoricalsociety.org; 678 Mission St; adult/child $5/free; gallery & store 11am-5pm Tue-Sun, library noon-5pm Wed-Fri; ; M Montgomery, B Montgomery)

TINNAPORN SATHAPORNNANONT/SHUTTERSTOCK ©

The Goddess of Victory statue, by Robert Ingersoll Aitken, atop the Dewey Monument

49 Geary GALLERY

5 Map p82, E2

Pity the collectors silently nibbling endive in austere Chelsea galleries – at 49 Geary, openings mean unexpected art, popcorn and outspoken crowds. Four floors of galleries feature standout international and local works, including photography at Fraenkel Gallery and Scott Nichols Gallery, Ai Weiwei installations at Haines Gallery, and Christian Maychack's architectural excess at Gregory Lind. For quieter contemplation, visit weekdays. (www.sfada.com; 49 Geary St; admission free; 10:30am-5:30pm Tue-Fri, 11am-5pm Sat; 5, 6, 7, 9, 21, 31, 38, M Powell, B Powell)

Children's Creativity Museum MUSEUM

6 Map p82, E3

No velvet ropes or hands-off signs here: kids rule, with high-tech displays double-daring them to make music videos, film claymation movies and construct play castles. Jump into live-action video games and sign up for workshops with Bay Area superstar animators, techno whizzes and robot builders. For low-tech fun, take a spin on the vintage-1906 **Loof Carousel** outside, operating 10am to 5pm daily; one $4 ticket covers two rides ($1 discount with museum admission). (415-820-3320; http://creativity.org/; 221 4th St; $12; 10am-4pm Wed-Sun; ; 14, M Powell, B Powell)

Eating

Benu

CALIFORNIAN, FUSION $$$

7  Map p82, F3

SF has pioneered Asian fusion cuisine for 150 years, but the pan-Pacific innovation chef-owner Corey Lee brings to the plate is gasp-inducing: foie-gras soup dumplings – what?! Dungeness crab and truffle custard pack such outsize flavor into Lee's faux-shark's fin soup, you'll swear Jaws is in there. Benu dinners are investments, but don't miss star sommelier Yoon Ha's ingenious pairings ($185). (415-685-4860; www.benusf.com; 22 Hawthorne St; tasting menu $285; 6-9pm seatings Tue-Sat; 10, 12, 14, 30, 45)

Top Tip

Top Tips

Make reservations whenever possible for downtown restaurants. Downtown and South of Market (SoMa) are best known for high-end restaurants, but lunchtime eateries in the neighborhood cater to office workers, with meals around $12 to $25. The Financial District is dead at night, when only midrange and top-end joints stay open. The Tenderloin (west of Powell St, south of Geary St, north of Market St) feels sketchy and rough but, as always in San Francisco, bargain eats reward the adventurous. Some cheap eateries in the 'Loin close earlier than their posted hours.

Tout Sweet

BAKERY $

8  Map p82, E2

Mango with Thai chili or peanut butter and jelly? Choosing your favorite California-French macaron isn't easy at Tout Sweet, where *Top Chef Just Desserts* champion Yigit Pura keeps outdoing his own inventions – he's like the love child of Julia Child and Steve Jobs. Chef Pura's sweet retreat on Macy's 3rd floor offers unbeatable views overlooking Union Sq, excellent teas and free wi-fi. (415-385-1679; www.toutsweetsf.com; Macy's, 3rd fl, cnr Geary & Stockton Sts; baked goods $2-8; 11am-6pm Sun-Wed, to 8pm Thu-Sat; ; 2, 38, Powell-Mason, Powell-Hyde, B Powell)

Kusakabe

SUSHI, JAPANESE $$$

9  Map p82, G1

Trust chef Mitsunori Kusakabe's *omakase* (tasting menu). Sit at the counter while chef adds a herbal hint to fatty tuna with the *inside* of a *shiso* leaf. After you devour the menu – mostly with your hands, 'to release flavors' – you can special-order Hokkaido sea urchin, which chef perfumes with the *outside* of the *shiso* leaf. Soy sauce isn't provided – or missed. (415-757-0155; http://kusakabe-sf.com; 584 Washington St; prix fixe $95; 5-10pm, last seating 8:30pm; 8, 10, 12, 41)

Sentinel

SANDWICHES $

10  Map p82, F3

Rebel SF chef Dennis Leary revolutionizes the humble sandwich with

top-notch seasonal ingredients: lamb gyros get radical with pesto and eggplant, and corned beef crosses borders with Swiss cheese and housemade Russian dressing. Check the website for daily menus and call in your order, or expect a 10-minute wait – sandwiches are made to order. Go to nearby **Yerba Buena Gardens** (415-820-3550; www.yerbabuenagardens.com; cnr 3rd & Mission Sts) to enjoy them. (415-284-9960; www.thesentinelsf.com; 37 New Montgomery St; sandwiches $9-12; 7:30am-2:30pm Mon-Fri; 12, 14, M Montgomery, B Montgomery)

Boulevard

CALIFORNIAN **$$$**

11 Map p82, H3

The 1889 belle epoque Audiffred Building once housed the Coast Seamen's Union, but for 20-plus years James Beard Award–winning chef Nancy Oakes has made culinary history here. Reliably tasty, effortlessly elegant dishes include juicy wood-oven-roasted Kurobuta pork chops, crisp California quail, and grilled Pacific salmon with wild morels, plus decadent, nostalgia-inducing cakes and ice cream, and SF's best service. (415-543-6084; www.boulevardrestaurant.com; 1 Mission St; mains lunch $15-29, dinner $29-51; 11:30am-2pm & 5:30-9:30pm Mon-Thu, to 10pm Fri, 5:30-10pm Sat, 5:30-9:30pm Sun; M Embarcadero, B Embarcadero)

Sushirrito

JAPANESE, FUSION **$**

12 Map p82, F2

Ever get a sushi craving, but you're hungry enough for a burrito? Join the crowd at Sushirrito, where fresh Latin and Asian ingredients are rolled in rice and nori seaweed, then conveniently wrapped in foil. Pan-Pacific Rim flavors shine in Geisha's Kiss, with line-caught yellowfin tuna and *piquillo* peppers, and vegetarian Buddha Belly, with spicy Japanese eggplant, kale and avocado. (415-544-9868; www.sushirrito.com; 226 Kearny St; dishes $9-13; 11am-4pm Mon-Thu, to 7pm Fri & Sat; ; 30, 45, B Montgomery, M Montgomery)

Tropisueño

MEXICAN **$$**

13 Map p82, E3

Last time you enjoyed casual Mexican dining this much, there were probably balmy ocean breezes and hammocks involved. Instead, you're steps away from SoMa museums, savoring *al pastor* (marinated pork) burritos with mesquite salsa and grilled pineapple, and sipping margaritas with chili-salted rims. Despite the prime downtown location, prices are down to earth – especially during happy hour (4pm to 6pm). (415-243-0299; www.tropisueno.com; 75 Yerba Buena Lane; mains lunch $7-12, dinner $12-21; 10am-10pm Sun-Thu, to 10:30pm Fri & Sat, 11am-10pm Sun; 8, 14, 30, 45, M Powell, B Powell)

Drinking

Bar Agricole

BAR

14 Map p82, A4

Drink your way to a history degree with well-researched cocktails: Whiz Bang with house bitters, whiskey, vermouth and absinthe scores high, but El Presidente with white rum, farmhouse curaçao and California-pomegranate grenadine takes top honors. This overachiever wins James Beard Award nods for spirits and eco-savvy design, plus popular acclaim for $1 oysters and $5 aperitifs 5pm to 6pm Monday to Saturday. (415-355-9400; www.baragricole.com; 355 11th St; 6-10pm Mon-Thu, 5:30-11pm Fri & Sat, 10am-2pm & 6-9pm Sun; 9, 12, 27, 47)

Local Edition

BAR

15 Map p82, E2

Get the scoop on the SF cocktail scene at this speakeasy in the basement of the historic Hearst newspaper building. The lighting is so dim you might bump into typewriters, but that's no excuse to dodge a Good Question: a cocktail of hibiscus-infused sherry, genever, thyme, salt, pepper and mystery. Book tables ahead for swinging live-music nights (Tuesday to Thursday). (415-795-1375; www.localeditionsf.com; 691 Market St; 5pm-2am Mon-Thu, from 4:30pm Fri, from 7pm Sat; M Montgomery, B Montgomery)

Rickhouse

BAR

16 Map p82, F2

Like a shotgun shack plunked downtown, Rickhouse is lined floor to ceiling with repurposed whiskey casks imported from Kentucky and back-bar shelving from an Ozarks nunnery that once secretly brewed hooch. Cocktails are strong on whiskey and bourbon – but the Californio with gold-dust bitters does rye proud. Round up a posse to help finish that vast bowl of Admiral's Whiskey Punch. (415-398-2827; www.rickhousebar.com; 246 Kearny St; 5pm-2am Mon, 3pm-2am Tue-Fri, 6pm-2am Sat; 8, 30, 45, M Montgomery, B Montgomery)

Cat Club

CLUB

17 Map p82, B4

You never really know your friends till you've seen them belt out A-ha's 'Take on Me' at Class of '84, Cat Club's Thursday-night retro dance party, where the euphoric bi/straight/gay/undefinable scene seems like an outtake from some John Hughes art-school flick. Tuesdays it's free karaoke, Wednesdays Bondage-a-Go-Go, Fridays Goth and Saturdays '80s and '90s power pop – dress the part and rock out.

Discounted admission before 10pm weekends. (www.sfcatclub.com; 1190 Folsom St; free-$12; 9pm-3am Tue-Sat; 12, 19, 27, 47, M Civic Center, B Civic Center)

Bloodhound

BAR

18 Map p82, B4

The murder of crows painted on the ceiling is an omen: nights at Bloodhound often assume mythic proportions. Vikings would feel at home amid these antler chandeliers, while bootleggers would appreciate barnwood walls and top-shelf hooch served in mason jars. Shoot pool or chill on leather couches until your jam comes on the jukebox. (415-863-2840; www.bloodhoundsf.com; 1145 Folsom St; 4pm-2am; 12, 14, 19, 27, 47)

Eagle Tavern

GAY, BAR

19 Map p82, A4

Sunday afternoons, all roads in the gay underground lead to the historic Eagle for all-you-can-drink beer busts ($15) from 3pm to 6pm. Wear leather – or flirt shamelessly – and blend right in; arrive before 3pm to beat long lines and score free BBQ. Thursdays bring mixed crowds for rockin' bands; Fridays and Saturdays range from bondage to drag. Check online. (www.sf-eagle.com; 398 12th St; $5-10; 2pm-2am Mon-Fri, from noon Sat & Sun; 9, 12, 27, 47)

Irish Bank

PUB

20 Map p82, F2

Perfectly pulled pints and thick-cut fries with malt vinegar are staples at this cozy Irish pub, hidden inside an alleyway near the Chinatown gate. Settle into your snug for juicy burgers, brats and anything else you could want with lashings of mustard. Sociable tables beneath the alley awning are ideal for easy banter and stigma-free smoking – rare in California. (415-788-7152; www.theirishbank.com; 10 Mark Lane; 11:30am-2am; 2, 3, 30, 45, M Montgomery, B Montgomery)

Hotel Utah Saloon (p91)

EndUp

GAY, CLUB

21 Map p82, C4

Forget Golden Gate Bridge – once you EndUp watching the sunrise over the 101 freeway ramp, you've officially arrived in SF. Dance sessions are marathons fueled by EndUp's

24-hour license, so Saturday nights have a way of turning into Monday mornings. Straight people sometimes EndUp here – but the gay Sunday tea dances have been legendary since 1973. Laughable bathrooms; serious weapon/drug checks. (☎415-646-0999; www.facebook.com/theendup; 401 6th St; $10-25; ⏰11pm Fri-8am Sat, 10pm Sat-4am Mon; 🚌12, 19, 27, 47)

Local Life

Giants Game Seats

The downside of the Giants' winning streak is that **Giants** (Map p82, F5; AT&T Park; ☎415-972-2000, tours 415-972-2400; http://sanfrancisco.giants.mlb.com; 24 Willie Mays Plaza; tickets $14-349, stadium tour adult/child/senior $22/12/17; ⏰tours 10:30am & 12.30pm; 👪; Ⓜ N, T) games often sell out, even though the stadium is among America's most expensive ballparks – the average cost for a family of four, including hot dogs and beer, is $239. Don't despair: season-ticket holders sell unwanted tickets through the team's Double Play Ticket Window (see http://sanfrancisco.giants.mlb.com).

If you can't find tickets, head to the park's eastern side along the waterfront, where you may be able to stand at the archways and watch innings for free. You'll need to show up hours early with die-hard local fans for a decent view – or be prepared to just glimpse the game and enjoy the party instead. Go Giants!

Entertainment

American Conservatory Theater

THEATER

22 Map p82, D1

Breakthrough shows launch at this turn-of-the-century landmark, which has hosted ACT's productions of Tony Kushner's *Angels in America* and Robert Wilson's *Black Rider*, with William S Burroughs' libretto and music by Tom Waits. Major playwrights like Tom Stoppard, Dustin Lance Black, Eve Ensler and David Mamet premiere work here, while the ACT's new **Strand Theater** (☎415-749-2228; www.act-sf.org/home/box_office/strand.html; 1127 Market St; 🚋F, Ⓑ Civic Center, Ⓜ Civic Center) stages experimental works. (ACT; ☎415-749-2228; www.act-sf.org; 405 Geary St; ⏰box office 10am-6pm Mon, to curtain Tue-Sun; 🚌8, 30, 38, 45, 🚋Powell-Mason, Powell-Hyde, Ⓑ Powell, Ⓜ Powell)

Oasis

CABARET

23 Map p82, A4

Forget what you've learned about drag on TV – at this dedicated dragstravaganza venue, the shows are so fearless, freaky-deaky and funny you'll laugh until it stops hurting. In a former gay bathhouse, drag-legendary owners Heklina and D'Arcy Drollinger mount original shows (sometimes literally), host drag-star DJs like Sharon Needles, and perform *Star Trek*, *Three's Company* and *Sex and the City* in drag. (☎415-795-3180; www.sfoasis.com; 298 11th St; tickets $15-35; 🚌9, 12, 14, 47, Ⓜ Van Ness)

Slim's

LIVE MUSIC

24 Map p82, A4

Guaranteed good times by Gogol Bordello, New Found Glory, Shiny Toy Guns and female Stones tribute band Chick Jagger fit the bill at this intimate club, owned by R&B star Boz Scaggs. Shows are all-ages, though shorties may have a hard time seeing once the floor starts bouncing. Reserve dinner for an additional $25 to score balcony seats. (415-255-0333; www.slimspresents.com; 333 11th St; tickets $15-30; box office 10:30am-6pm Mon-Fri & show nights; 9, 12, 27, 47)

Hotel Utah Saloon

LIVE MUSIC

25 Map p82, D5

This Victorian saloon ruled SF's '70s underground scene, when upstarts Whoopi Goldberg and Robin Williams took to the stage – and fresh talents surface here during Monday open-mike nights, indie-label debuts and twangy weekend showcases. In the '50s the bartender graciously served Beats and drifters but snipped off suits' ties; now you can wear whatever, but there's a $20 credit-card minimum. (415-546-6300; www.hotelutah.com; 500 4th St; free-$10; 11:30am-2am; 30, 47, M N, T)

DNA Lounge

LIVE PERFORMANCE

26 Map p82, A4

SF's reigning megaclub hosts bands, literary slams and big-name DJs, with two floors of late-night dance action just seedy enough to be interesting. Original Saturday mash-up party Bootie brings Justin/Justin (Bieber/Timberlake) jams; Fridays are for Hubba-Hubba Burlesque revues and writers reading teenage diaries at Mortified; Mondays mean Goth/industrial bands at 18-plus Death Guild. Check calendar; early arrivals may hear crickets. (415-626-1409; www.dnalounge.com; 375 11th St; $9-35; 9pm-5am; 9, 12, 27, 47)

Top Tip

Tickets on the Cheap

Score half-price seats for unsold day-of (or next-day) shows at **TIX Bay Area** (Map p82, E2; http://tixbayarea.org; 350 Powell St; Powell-Mason, Powell-Hyde, B Powell, M Powell), Union Sq's discount-ticket booth. Check the website first, because some tickets are available only online, and others only at the booth.

Mezzanine

LIVE MUSIC

27 Map p82, D3

Big nights come with bragging rights at Mezzanine, with one of the city's best sound systems and crowds hyped for breakthrough shows by hip-hop greats like Wyclef and Mystikal, pop powerhouses like Lupe Fiasco, and Saturday Controvrsy dance-offs (spoiler alert for Rihanna-versus-Beyonce nights: B wins, every time). No in/out privileges. (415-625-8880; www.mezzaninesf.com; 444 Jessie St; $20-60; M Powell, B Powell)

Punch Line

COMEDY

28 Map p82, G1

Known for launching big talent (including Robin Williams, Chris Rock, Ellen DeGeneres and David Cross), this historic stand-up venue is small enough for you to hear sighs of relief backstage when jokes kill, and teeth grind when they bomb. Strong drinks loosen up the crowd, but you might not be laughing tomorrow. (415-397-7573; www.punchlinecomedyclub.com; 444 Battery St; $15-25, plus 2-drink minimum; shows 8pm Tue-Thu & Sun, 8pm & 10pm Fri, 7:30pm & 9:30pm Sat; M Embarcadero, B Embarcadero)

> Local Life
>
> **Downtown Rooftop Gardens**
>
> Above the busy sidewalks, there's a serene world of unmarked public rooftop gardens that grant perspective on downtown's skyscraper canyons. They're called 'privately owned public-open spaces' (POPOs). Local public-advocacy urbanist group **SPUR** (415-781-8726; www.spur.org; 654 Mission St; admission free; 11am-5pm Tue-Fri; 12, 14, B Montgomery, M Montgomery) publishes a downloadable app that lists them all. Local favorites:
>
> **One Montgomery Terrace** (Map p82, E2; 50 Post St/1 Montgomery St; 10am-6pm Mon-Sat; M Montgomery, B Montgomery) has great Market St views of old and new SF. Enter through Crocker Galleria, take the elevator to the top, then ascend the stairs; or enter Wells Fargo at One Montgomery and take the elevator to 'R.'
>
> **Sun Terrace** (Map p82, G2; 343 Sansome St; 10am-6pm Mon-Fri; M Embarcadero, B Embarcadero) has knockout vistas of the Financial District and Transamerica Pyramid from atop a slender art-deco skyscraper. Take the elevator to the 15th floor.

Shopping

Recchiuti Chocolates

FOOD & DRINKS

29 Map p82, H2

No San Franciscan can resist award-winning Recchiuti: Pacific Heights parts with old money for its *fleur de sel* caramels; Noe Valley's foodie kids prefer S'more Bites to the campground variety; North Beach toasts to the red-wine-pairing chocolate box; and the Mission approves SF-landmark chocolates designed by Creativity Explored – proceeds benefit the Mission arts-education nonprofit for artists with developmental disabilities. (415-834-9494; www.recchiuticonfections.com; 1 Ferry Bldg, cnr Market St & the Embarcadero; 10am-7pm Mon-Fri, 8am-6pm Sat, 10am-5pm Sun; M Embarcadero, B Embarcadero)

Britex Fabrics

ARTS & CRAFTS

30  Map p82, E2

Runways can't compete with Britex' fashion drama since 1952. First floor:

Understand

Bay Bridge

Artist Leo Villareal's installation of twinkling lights along the western span will make you swear the Bay Bridge (www.baybridgeinfo.org) is winking at you. In 2013 Villareal strung 25,000 lights along the Bay Bridge's vertical suspension cables, transforming the 1.8-mile western span into the world's largest and most psychedelic LED display.

The Bay Bridge Lights blink in never-repeating patterns – one second the bridge looks like bubbly champagne, then a lava-lamp forest, then Vegas-style swaying fountains. You could stare at it for hours...hopefully not while driving. The installation was meant to be temporary, but thanks to local donors, it was permanently installed in 2016.

designers bicker over dibs on caution-orange chiffon. Second floor: glam rockers dig through velvet goldmines. Third floor: Hollywood costumers make vampire-movie magic with jet buttons and hand-dyed ribbon. Top floor: fake fur flies and remnants roll as costumers prepare for Burning Man, Halloween and your average SF weekend. (415-392-2910; www.britexfabrics.com; 146 Geary St; 10am-6pm Mon-Sat; 38, Powell-Mason, Powell-Hyde, M Powell, B Powell)

San Francisco Railway Museum Gift Shop GIFTS & SOUVENIRS

31 Map p82, H3

The next best thing to taking an SF cable car home with you is getting a scale-model streetcar from this tiny, free Municipal Railway museum showcasing SF public transit. Earn instant SF street cred with baseball caps and T-shirts emblazoned with Muni slogans, including everyone's favorite: 'Information gladly given, but safety requires avoiding unnecessary conversation.' (415-974-1948; www.streetcar.org/museum; 77 Steuart St; 10am-5pm Tue-Sun; Embarcadero, B Embarcadero)

Mr S Leather ADULT

32 Map p82, B4

Only in San Francisco would you find an S&M superstore, with such musts as suspension stirrups, latex hoods and, for that special someone, a chrome-plated codpiece. If you've been a very bad puppy, there's an entire doghouse department catering to you here, and gluttons for punishment will find home-decor inspiration in dungeon furniture. (415-863-7764; www.mr-s-leather.com; 385 8th St; 11am-8pm; 12, 19, 27, 47)

Explore

Hayes Valley & Civic Center

Don't be fooled by its grand formality – San Francisco's Civic Center is down-to-earth and cutting edge. City Hall helped launch gay rights and green schemes, and arts institutions nearby ensure San Francisco is never lost for inspiration. West of City Hall lies Hayes Valley, where jazz accompanies skateboarders, Victorian buildings showcase upstart designers and creative crowds socialize in shipping containers.

The Sights in a Day

Get a fresh start at **farm:table** (p103), then hop the historic F-line streetcar to the **Asian Art Museum** (p96). Here you'll cover the Silk Road in an hour, from Persian miniatures to Chinese snuff bottles. Across the plaza at **City Hall** (p100), you can see where sit-ins, gay marriage and zero-waste mandates made US history.

Browse boutiques down Hayes St to sensational **Souvla** (p103) salads, followed by curbside **Blue Bottle Coffee** (p104). Hit the comics lounge at **Isotope** (p109), get fog-dewy skin at **Nancy Boy** (p108) and try SF history on for size at **Paloma** (p108).

Haul your booty to pirate-themed speakeasy **Smuggler's Cove** (p105) – but don't let that Dead Reckoning cocktail delay dinner at **Rich Table** (p102) or your grand entrance at **San Francisco Symphony** (p107), **San Francisco Opera** (p107) or **SFJAZZ** (p106). End your night in a compromising position at **Hemlock Tavern** (p108), and you've done SF proud.

Top Sight

Asian Art Museum (p96)

Best of San Francisco

Live Music

SFJAZZ Center (p106)

San Francisco Symphony (p107)

San Francisco Opera (p107)

Great American Music Hall (p107)

Warfield (p108)

Drinks

Smuggler's Cove (p105)

Bourbon & Branch (p106)

Hemlock Tavern (p108)

Rye (p105)

Blue Bottle Coffee (p104)

Getting There

Streetcar Historic F Market streetcars run along Market St; J, K, L, M and N metro lines run under Market St to Van Ness and Civic Center stations.

Bus Lines 2, 5, 6, 7, 21 and 31 run down Market to Civic Center toward Hayes Valley; lines 47 and 49 run along Van Ness.

Car Garage under Civic Center Plaza.

Top Sights
Asian Art Museum

Sightsee halfway across the globe in an hour, from romantic Persian miniatures to daring Chinese installation art – just don't go bumping into those priceless Ming vases. The museum's curators work diplomatic wonders here, bringing Taiwan, China and Tibet together, uniting Pakistan and India, and reconciling Japan, Korea and China under one Italianate roof. The distinguished collection of 18,000 unique treasures also does the city proud, reflecting San Francisco's 165-year history as North America's gateway to Asia.

Map p98, E4

415-581-3500

www.asianart.org

200 Larkin St

adult/student/child $15/10/free, 1st Sun of month free

10am-5pm Tue-Sun, to 9pm Thu

M Civic Center, B Civic Center

Asian Art Museum

Permanent Collection

The Asian Art Museum's curatorial concept is to follow the evolution of Asian art from West to East toward San Francisco, along Buddhist pilgrimage trails and trade routes. Granted, the Chinese collection takes up two wings and South Asia only one – but that healthy cultural competition has encouraged donations of South Asian artifacts lately.

Start your tour on the 3rd floor with a treasure trove of Indian miniatures and jewels. Detour through dizzying Iranian geometric tiles and Javanese shadow puppets, and turn a corner to find Tibetan prayer wheels. Ahead is a 3000-year-old Chinese bronze rhinoceros wine vessel with a twinkle in its eye, plus Chinese jades and snuff bottles. Downstairs on the 2nd floor are calligraphy, Korean celadon bowls and an entire Japanese-tea-ceremony room.

Contemporary Shows

As you wander through 6000 years of Asian art, look for artworks by contemporary artists responding to pieces in the collection. Rotating ground-floor exhibits spotlight exceptional collections and groundbreaking artists. Artists Drawing Club events held upstairs in Samsung Hall invite visitors to collaborate in a contemporary artist's art-making process.

Architecture

Italian architect Gae Aulenti's clever repurposing of the old San Francisco Main Library building left intact the much-beloved granite bas-relief on the building's facade, travertine entry arches and the grand stone staircase. She added two new indoor courts for oversize installations, leaving plenty of room for debate and educational programs.

Top Tips

- On Thursday nights (5pm to 9pm, February through September), the Asian gets hip with cross-cultural mash-up DJs and special guests – lately, Asian American slam poets, Korean quilters, and Olympian martial artists kicking with lethal force.
- Parents can pick up Explorer Cards for kids to find favorite animals and characters in the galleries.
- Check the schedule for live artists' demonstrations, free yoga classes and hands-on workshops for kids.

Take a Break

On the museum's sunny terrace at **Café Asia** (www.asianart.org/visit/cafe-asia; 200 Larkin St; mains $5-14; 10am-4:30pm Tue-Sun, to 8:30pm Thu Feb-Oct; ; 5,6,7,21, M Civic Center), enjoy tea-smoked Pacific salmon with soba noodles.

A
B
C
D
1
2
3
4
5
For reviews see
Top Sights p96
Sights p100
Eating p102
Drinking p104
Entertainment p106
Shopping p108
WESTERN ADDITION
Eddy St
Ellis St
Gough St
Turk St
Jefferson Square
Hayward Playground
Golden Gate Ave
Franklin St
McAllister St
Octavia St
Elm St
Larch St
Buchanan St
Fulton St
Birch St
Laguna St
Grove St
Ivy St
Hayes St
Linden St
Redwood St
McAllister St
War Memorial Opera House
Gough St
Franklin St
City Hall
Patricia's Green
HAYES VALLEY
Dr Carlton B Goodlett Pl
Civic Center Plaza
Page St
Fell St
Hayes St
Grove St
Rose St
Hickory St
Van Ness Ave
Ivy St
Haight St
Octavia Blvd
Oak St
Lily St
CIVIC CENTER
Market St
Van Ness
McCoppin St
Colton St
12th St
11th St
10th St
9th St
Otis St
Mission St
1
6
7
8
11
13
14
16
19
20
21
22
26
27
28
29

E
F
G
H
1
2
3
4
5
0
400 m
0
0.2 miles
Geary Blvd
Hemlock St
24
Cedar St
Polk St
Van Ness Ave
Myrtle St
Larkin St
18
Olive St
23
Willow St
THE TENDERLOIN
Bush St
Pine St
Sutter St
Hyde St
Post St
Leavenworth St
Geary St
10
9
17
Cosmo Pl
Post St
Jones St
12
O'Farrell St
Ellis St
Eddy St
Polk St
Larkin St
Shannon St
Tenderloin Museum Walking Tours
5
Glide Memorial United Methodist Church
4
Taylor St
Hyde St
Turk St
Leavenworth St
Golden Gate Ave
Ellis St
Mason St
Asian Art Museum
Eddy St
3
San Francisco Main Library
McAllister St
Jones St
15
Powell St Cable Car Turnaround
United Nations Plaza
25
Market St
Civic Center
2
Luggage Store Gallery
UNION SQUARE
Stevenson St
8th St
Jessie St
7th St
6th St
5th St
Mission St

Sights

City Hall
HISTORIC BUILDING

1 Map p98, D3

Rising from the ashes of the 1906 earthquake, this beaux arts landmark echoes with history. Demonstrators protesting red-scare McCarthy hearings on City Hall steps in 1960 were blasted with fire hoses – yet America's first sit-in worked. America's first openly gay official supervisor, Harvey Milk, was assassinated here in 1978, along with Mayor George Moscone – but, in 2004, 4037 same-sex couples were legally wed here. Recently, City Hall has made headlines for approving pioneering environmental initiatives and citywide sanctuary status. (tour info 415-554-6139; http://sfgov.org/cityhall/city-hall; 400 Van Ness Ave; admission free; 8am-8pm Mon-Fri, tours 10am, noon & 2pm; ; M Civic Center, B Civic Center)

Top Tip

Street Smarts

Most first-time visitors are surprised to find that merely by crossing touristy Powell St or busy Van Ness Ave, they enter the down-and-out Tenderloin. Keep your street smarts about you in the area bounded by Powell and Geary to the north, Mission St to the south and Polk St to the west. When possible, avoid these sketchy blocks, take public transit or cabs through the area, or walk briskly along Geary or Market Sts to reach specific destinations.

Luggage Store Gallery
GALLERY

2 Map p98, G5

Like a dandelion pushing through sidewalk cracks, this plucky nonprofit gallery has brought signs of life to one of the Tenderloin's toughest blocks for two decades. By giving SF street artists a gallery platform, the Luggage Store helped launch graffiti-art star Barry McGee, muralist Rigo and street photographer Cheryl Dunn. Find the graffitied door and climb to the 2nd-floor gallery, which rises above the street without losing sight of it. (415-255-5971; www.luggagestoregallery.org; 1007 Market St; noon-5pm Wed-Sat; 5, 6, 7, 21, 31, M Civic Center, B Civic Center)

San Francisco Main Library
CULTURAL CENTER

3 Map p98, E4

A grand light well illuminates SF's favorite subjects: poetry in the Robert Frost Collection, civil rights in the Hormel LGBTQIA Center, SF music zines in the Little Maga/Zine Center and comic relief in the Schmulowitz Collection of Wit and Humor. Check out the 2nd-floor wallpaper made from the old card catalog – artists Ann Chamberlain and Ann Hamilton invited 200 San Franciscans to add multilingual commentary to 50,000 cards. The library quietly hosts high-profile basement lectures, plus enlightening Skylight Gallery ephemera exhibits.

NICKOLAY STANEV/SHUTTERSTOCK ©

City Hall illuminated in rainbow colors for Pride Week

(☎415-557-4400; www.sfpl.org; 100 Larkin St; admission free; ⏰10am-6pm Mon & Sat, 9am-8pm Tue-Thu, noon-6pm Fri, noon-5pm Sun; 👪; 🚌5, 6, 7, 19, 21, 31, Ⓜ Civic Center, Ⓑ Civic Center)

Glide Memorial United Methodist Church CHURCH

4 👁 Map p98, G3

When the rainbow-robed Glide gospel choir enters singing their hearts out, the 2000-plus congregation erupts in cheers, hugs and dance moves. Raucous Sunday Glide celebrations capture San Francisco at its most welcoming and uplifting, embracing the rainbow spectrum of culture, gender, orientation, ability and socioeconomics. After the celebration ends, the congregation keeps the inspiration coming, serving a million free meals a year and providing housing for 52 formerly homeless families – and, yes, Glide welcomes volunteers. (☎415-674-6090; www.glide.org; 330 Ellis St; ⏰celebrations 9am & 11am Sun; 👪; 🚌38, Ⓜ Powell, Ⓑ Powell)

Tenderloin Museum Walking Tours WALKING

5 👁 Map p98, G3

The Tenderloin's notoriety as a red-light district keeps tourists from witnessing historic sites where Muhammad Ali boxed, Miles Davis recorded, and LGBT activists fought for their right to be served in cafeterias – and

established America's first Transgender Historic District. Resident Tenderloin Museum historians lead intrepid visitors past these and other groundbreaking Tenderloin locales; walking shoes and city smarts essential. (415-351-1912; www.tenderloinmuseum.org/tours; 398 Eddy St; adult/with museum admission/night tour $10/15/17; 11am & 2pm Tue-Sat, 2pm Sun, 21+ night tour 6pm Wed; B Powell, M Powell, Powell-Mason, Powell-Hyde)

Local Life

Twitter's Controversial HQ

Market St's 1937 Mayan deco landmark once housed 300 furniture showrooms – but a decade ago, less than 30 remained. The city offered controversial tax incentives to Twitter to keep its HQ in SF, and after a $1.2 million LEED-certified green makeover, Twitter nested here. Only employees can access Twitter's free cafeteria, but you can buy local gourmet fare at the ground-floor **Marketplace** (Map p98, D5; Western Furniture Exchange & Merchandise Mart; https://about.twitter.com/company; 1355 Market St; 6, 7, 21, M Civic Center, B Civic Center). Meanwhile, artists demanded to know: if tech gets tax breaks, what would SF offer the arts to stay? Finally, the city cut a deal enabling arts nonprofits to buy Market St storefronts, including **Luggage Store Gallery** (p100), **SF Camerawork** (Map p98, G5; 415-487-1011; www.sfcamerawork.org; 1011 Market St, 2nd fl; admission free; noon-6pm Tue-Sat; 6, 7, 9, 21, B Civic Center, M Civic Center) and **Root Division** (Map p98, F5; 415-863-7668; www.rootdivision.org; 1131 Mission St; donations welcome; gallery 2-6pm Wed-Sat; ; 6, 9, 71, B Civic Center, streetcar F, M Civic Center).

Eating

Rich Table

CALIFORNIAN **$$$**

6 Map p98, B4

Impossible cravings begin at Rich Table, inventor of porcini doughnuts, miso-marrow-stuffed pasta and fried-chicken madeleines with caviar. Married cochefs and owners Sarah and Evan Rich playfully riff on seasonal California fare, freestyling with whimsical off-menu amuse-bouches like trippy beet marshmallows or the Dirty Hippie: nutty hemp atop silky goat-buttermilk *pannacotta*, as offbeat and entrancing as Hippie Hill drum circles. (415-355-9085; http://richtablesf.com; 199 Gough St; mains $17-30; 5:30-10pm Sun-Thu, to 10:30pm Fri & Sat; 5, 6, 7, 21, 47, 49, M Van Ness)

Jardinière

CALIFORNIAN **$$$**

7 Map p98, C3

Iron Chef winner, *Top Chef Masters* finalist and James Beard Award–winner Traci Des Jardins champions sustainable, salacious California cuisine. She has a way with California's organic produce, sustainable meats and seafood that's probably illegal in other states, slathering sturgeon with buttery chanterelles and lavishing root vegetables with truffles and honey

from Jardinière's rooftop hives. Mondays bring $55 three-course dinners with wine pairings. (☎415-861-5555; www.jardiniere.com; 300 Grove St; mains $20-36; ⏲5-9pm Sun-Thu, to 10:30pm Fri & Sat; 🚌5, 21, 47, 49, Ⓜ Van Ness)

Souvla

GREEK $

Map p98, B3

Ancient Greek philosophers didn't think too hard about lunch, and neither should you at Souvla's. Get in line and make no-fail choices: pita or salad, wine or not. Instead of go-to gyros, try roast lamb atop kale with yogurt dressing, or tangy chicken salad with pickled onion and *mizithra* cheese. Go early/late for skylit communal seating, or head to **Patricia's Green** (http://proxysf.net; cnr Octavia Blvd & Fell St; 🚌5, 21) with takeout. (☎415-400-5458; www.souvlasf.com; 517 Hayes St; sandwiches & salads $11-14; ⏲11am-10pm; 🚌5, 21, 47, 49, Ⓜ Van Ness)

farm:table

AMERICAN $

Map p98, H2

A ray of sunshine in the concrete heart of the city, this plucky little storefront showcases seasonal California organics in just-baked breakfasts and farmstead-fresh lunches. Check the menu on Twitter (@farmtable) for today's homemade cereals, savory tarts and game-changing toast – mmmm, ginger peach and mascarpone on whole-wheat sourdough. Tiny space, but immaculate kitchen and great coffee. Cash only. (☎415-292-7089; www.farmtablesf.com; 754 Post St; dishes $6-9; ⏲7:30am-2pm Tue-Fri, 8am-3pm Sat & Sun; 🌱; 🚌2, 3, 27, 38)

Local Life

Heart of the City Farmers Market

The savviest wheeler-dealers aren't in City Hall – they're over at the **farmers market** (Map p98, E4; www.hotcfarmersmarket.org; United Nations Plaza; ⏲7am-5:30pm Wed, to 5pm Sun; 👪; 🚌6, 7, 9, 21, Ⓜ Civic Center, Ⓑ Civic Center), where California producers set up shop in the UN Plaza amid the usual skateboarders, Scientologists and raving self-talkers. These stands yield heirloom organic raspberries for $2 a pint and cold-filtered virgin olive oil for $9 a bottle. Off the Grid food trucks pull up alongside, selling roast chicken with lavender salt and warm maple-bacon doughnuts.

Liholiho Yacht Club

HAWAIIAN, CALIFORNIAN $$

Map p98

Who needs yachts to be happy? Aloha abounds over Liholiho's pucker-up-tart cocktails and gleefully creative Calwaiian/Hawafornian dishes – surefire mood enhancers include spicy beef-tongue *bao*, duck-liver mousse with pickled pineapple on brioche, and Vietnamese slaw with tender squid and crispy tripe. Reservations are impossible; arrive early/late for bar dining, or head downstairs to Louie's Gen-Gen

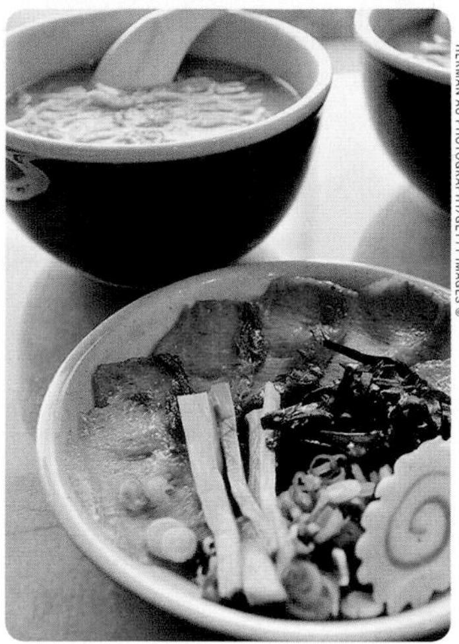
HERMAN AU PHOTOGRAPHY/GETTY IMAGES ©

Ramen

Room speakeasy for shamelessly tasty bone-marrow-butter waffles. (☎415-440-5446; http://lycsf.com; 871 Sutter St; dishes $11-37; ⏰5-10:30pm Mon-Thu, to 11pm Fri & Sat; 🚌2, 3, 27, 38, 🚋California)

Nojo Ramen Tavern JAPANESE $$

11 Map p98, C4

Find moments of clarity on foggy Hayes Valley nights with restorative, eye-opening bowls of proper ramen. Housemade broth brings bottomless flavor to modest bowls of noodles, topped by house-specialty chicken any way you want it – shredded, slow-braised, in meatballs or ground with spice. Get the optional 'spice bomb' and well-priced local beer and wine by the glass. (☎415-896-4587; www.nojosf.com; 231 Franklin St; noodle bowls $16-18.50; ⏰5-11pm Tue-Sat, 11:30am-2:30pm & 4-7pm Sun; 🚌5, 6, 7, 21, 47, 49, Ⓜ Van Ness)

Hooker's Sweet Treats DESSERTS

12 Map p98, F2

Bring your sweet tooth and twisted sense of humor – Hooker's name winks knowingly at other businesses conducted on nearby street corners, but the decadent desserts on offer are no joke. Get bread pudding for here and award-winning caramels to go – Town S'Mhore caramels tempt with marshmallows and pecans, but get 3rd Nut with fair-trade chocolate, pistachios and sea salt. (☎415-441-4628; www.hookerssweettreats.com; 442 Hyde St; ⏰8am-3pm Tue-Fri, 10am-2pm Sat; 🚌2, 3, 19, 27, 38, 47, 49)

Drinking

Blue Bottle Coffee Kiosk CAFE

13 Map p98, B3

Don't mock SF's coffee geekery until you've tried the elixir emerging from this back-alley garage-door kiosk. The Bay Area's Blue Bottle built its reputation with microroasted organic coffee – especially Blue Bottle–invented, off-the-menu Gibraltar, the barista-favorite drink with foam and espresso poured together into the eponymous short glass. Expect a (short) wait and seats outside on creatively repurposed traffic curbs.

(www.bluebottlecoffee.net; 315 Linden St; 7am-6pm Mon-Sat, from 8am Sun; ; 5, 21, 47, 49, M Van Ness)

Smuggler's Cove

BAR

14 Map p98, C3

Yo-ho-ho and a bottle of rum… wait, make that a Dead Reckoning (Nicaraguan rum, port, pineapple and bitters), unless you'll split the flaming Scorpion Bowl? Pirates are bedeviled by choice at this Barbary Coast–shipwreck tiki bar, hidden behind tinted-glass doors. With 550 rums and 70-plus cocktails gleaned from rum-running around the world – and $2 off 5pm to 6pm daily – you won't be dry-docked long. (415-869-1900; www.smugglerscovesf.com; 650 Gough St; 5pm-1:15am; 5, 21, 47, 49, M Civic Center, B Civic Center)

Aunt Charlie's Lounge

GAY, CLUB

15 Map p98, G4

Vintage pulp-fiction covers come to life when the Hot Boxxx Girls storm the battered stage at Aunt Charlie's on Friday and Saturday nights at 10pm ($5; call for reservations). Thursday is Tubesteak Connection ($5, free before 10pm), when bathhouse anthems and '80s disco draw throngs of art-school gays. Other nights bring guaranteed minor mayhem, seedy glamour and Tenderloin dive-bar shenanigans. (415-441-2922; www.auntcharlieslounge.com; 133 Turk St; free-$5; noon-2am Mon-Fri, from 10am Sat, 10am-midnight Sun; 27, 31, M Powell, B Powell)

Riddler

WINE BAR

16 Map p98, A3

Riddle me this: how can you ever thank the women in your life? As the Riddler's all-women sommelier-chef-investor team points out, champagne makes a fine start. Bubbles begin at $12 and include Veuve Cliquot, the brand named after the woman who invented riddling, the process that gives champagne its unclouded sparkle. (www.theriddlersf.com; 528 Laguna St; 4-10pm Sun & Tue-Thu, to 11pm Fri & Sat; 5, 6, 7, 21)

Rye

LOUNGE

17 Map p98, G2

Swagger into this sleek sunken lounge for cocktails that look sharp and pack more heat than Steve McQueen in *Bullitt*. The soundtrack is '80s and the drinks strictly old school – bartenders mix their own rye Pimm's No 5 Cup with ginger and proper English cucumber. Come early to sip at your leisure on leather couches and leave before the smokers' cage overflows. (415-474-4448; www.ryesf.com; 688 Geary St; 5:30pm-2am Mon-Fri, from 6pm Sat, from 7pm Sun; 2, 3, 27, 38)

Edinburgh Castle

PUB

18 Map p98, F2

Bagpiper murals on the walls, the *Trainspotting* soundtrack on the jukebox, ale on tap, Tuesday pub quiz and vinegary fish and chips until 9pm provide all the Scottish authenticity

you could ask for, short of haggis. This flag-waving bastion of drink comes fully equipped with dartboard, pool tables, DJs on Saturday and the Quiet Lightning reading series on Monday. (☎415-885-4074; www.thecastlesf.com; 950 Geary St; ⏲5pm-2am; 🚌19, 38, 47, 49)

Local Life

Bourbon & Branch

Some of the best cocktails you'll have in SF (or anywhere) are hiding in plain sight under a deliberately misleading Anti-Saloon League sign. **Bourbon & Branch** (Map p98, G3; ☎415-346-1735; www.bourbonandbranch.com; 501 Jones St; ⏲6pm-2am; 🚌27, 38) is an authentic re-creation of a Prohibition-era speakeasy, complete with secret exits and basement bullet holes from its heyday – only now the locally crafted spirits aren't made in a bathtub. For historically researched, highly original top-shelf gin and bourbon cocktails, give the bouncer the password ('books') and you'll be led through a bookcase secret passage to the most liquored-up **library** in America. 'Don't even think of asking for a cosmo' reads one of many posted House Rules here – but you can't go wrong with the Scofflaw (whiskey, vermouth, grenadine and housemade bitters). Reservations are required for front-room booths, and for **Wilson & Wilson Detective Agency**, the noir-themed speakeasy-within-a-speakeasy (password supplied with reservations). Keep it under your hat.

Rickshaw Stop

CLUB

19 Map p98, C4

Welcome to the high-school prom you always wanted: indie bands, DIY decor, glitter drag and '90s getups in a former TV studio. Regular events include Popscene indie bands, Brazilian breakbeat nights, Nerd Nite lecture mixers and monthly gay Asian house party GAMeBoi. Some nights welcome ages 18-plus, others 21-plus; doors open around 8pm and main acts kick off around 10pm. (☎415-861-2011; www.rickshawstop.com; 155 Fell St; $5-35; 🚌21, 47, 49, Ⓜ Van Ness)

Entertainment

SFJAZZ Center

JAZZ

20 Map p98, C4

Jazz legends and singular talents from Argentina to Yemen are showcased at America's newest, largest jazz center. Hear fresh takes on classic jazz albums and poets riffing with jazz combos in the downstairs Joe Henderson Lab, and witness extraordinary main-stage collaborations ranging from Afro-Cuban All Stars to roots legends Emmylou Harris, Rosanne Cash and Lucinda Williams.

Jazz-themed cocktails are served on the balcony, and you can take them into the LEED-certified glass-and-concrete auditorium – even upper-tier cheap seats have drink holders and clear stage views. Upstairs, test your knowledge of jazz history with Sandow Birk's tile

murals capturing the scene from coast to coast. Check the website for family matinees and master classes on subjects ranging from studio audio mixing to hip-hop jazz sampling. (☎866-920-5299; www.sfjazz.org; 201 Franklin St; tickets $25-120; 👪; 🚌5, 6, 7, 21, 47, 49, Ⓜ Van Ness)

San Francisco Symphony

CLASSICAL MUSIC

21 ★ Map p98, C4

From the moment conductor Michael Tilson Thomas bounces up on his toes and raises his baton, the audience is on the edge of their seats for another thunderous performance by the Grammy-winning SF Symphony. Don't miss signature concerts of Beethoven and Mahler, live symphony performances with such films as *Star Trek*, and creative collaborations with artists from Elvis Costello to Metallica. (☎box office 415-864-6000, rush-ticket hotline ☎415-503-5577; www.sfsymphony.org; Grove St, btwn Franklin St & Van Ness Ave; tickets $20-150; 🚌21, 45, 47, Ⓜ Van Ness, Ⓑ Civic Center)

San Francisco Opera

OPERA

22 ★ Map p98, C3

Opera was SF's gold-rush soundtrack – and SF Opera rivals the Met, with world premieres of original works ranging from Stephen King's *Dolores Claiborne* to *Girls of the Golden West*, filmmaker Peter Sellars' collaboration with composer John Adams. Expect haute couture costumes and radical sets by painter David Hockney. Score $10 same-day standing-room tickets

STEVE JENNINGS/GETTY IMAGES ©

Esperanza Spalding performing at the SFJAZZ Center

at 10am; check website for Opera Lab pop-ups. (☎415-864-3330; www.sfopera.com; War Memorial Opera House, 301 Van Ness Ave; tickets $10-350; 🚌21, 45, 47, Ⓑ Civic Center, Ⓜ Van Ness)

Great American Music Hall

LIVE MUSIC

23 ★ Map p98, F2

Everyone busts out their best sets at this opulent 1907 bordello turned all-ages venue – indie rockers like the Band Perry throw down, international legends like Salif Keita grace the stage, and John Waters hosts Christmas extravaganzas. Pay $25 extra for dinner with prime balcony seating

to watch shows comfortably, or rock out with the standing-room scrum downstairs. (415-885-0750; www.gamh.com; 859 O'Farrell St; shows $20-45; box office 10:30am-6pm Mon-Fri & show nights; ; 19, 38, 47, 49)

Hemlock Tavern

LIVE MUSIC

24 Map p98, F1

When you wake up tomorrow with peanut shells in your hair (weren't they on the floor?) and a stiff neck from rocking too hard to the Lucky Eejits (weren't they insane?), you'll know it was another successful, near-lethal night at the Hemlock. Blame it on cheap drink at the oval bar, pogo-worthy punk and a sociable smoker's room (yes, in California). (415-923-0923; www.hemlocktavern.com; 1131 Polk St; free-$10; 4pm-2am; 2, 3, 19, 47, 49)

Warfield

LIVE MUSIC

25 Map p98, G4

Big acts with international followings play this former vaudeville theater. Marquee names like Wu-Tang Clan, Iggy Pop, Kanye West and Sarah Silverman explain the line down this seedy Tenderloin block and the packed, pot-smoky balconies. Beer costs $9 to $10 and water $4, so you might as well get cocktails. Street parking isn't advisable – try the garage at 5th and Mission. (888-929-7849; www.thewarfieldtheatre.com; 982 Market St; box office 10am-4pm Sun & 90min before shows; M Powell, B Powell)

Shopping

Paloma

FASHION & ACCESSORIES

26 Map p98, B4

Like raiding a surrealist's attic, this SF maker collective yields highly unlikely, imaginatively reinvented finds. Don't be surprised to discover billiard-ball cocktail rings, hand-patched indigo scarves, or real buffalo nickels adorning handbags made on-site by artisan Laureano Faedi. On SF-history T-shirts, Faedi emblazons insignias from bizarre bygone businesses, from Playland at the Beach to Topsy's Roost, SF's chicken-themed speakeasy. (https://instagram.com/palomahayesvalley; 112 Gough St; noon-7pm Tue-Sat; 5, 6, 7, 21, 47, 49, M Van Ness)

Nancy Boy

COSMETICS

27 Map p98, C3

All you closet pomaders and after-sun balmers: wear those potions with pride, without feeling like the dupe of some cosmetics conglomerate. Clever Nancy Boy knows you'd rather pay for the product than for advertising campaigns featuring the starlet du jour, and delivers locally made wares with effective plant oils that are tested on boyfriends, never animals. (415-552-3636; www.nancyboy.com; 347 Hayes St; 11am-7pm Mon-Sat, to 6pm Sun; 5, 21, 47, 49)

Hemlock Tavern

Amour Vert FASHION & ACCESSORIES

28 Map p98, B3

Looking smart comes easy with effortless wardrobe essentials that casually blend style, comfort and sustainability. Wear your heart on your sleeve with feel-good fabrics ingeniously engineered from renewable sources, including Italian flax linen, eucalyptus-tree Tencel and Peruvian cooperative-grown organic cotton. Find soft, flattering pieces at down-to-earth prices, designed in San Francisco and US-made to last a lifetime. (415-800-8576; https://amourvert.com; 437 Hayes St; 11am-7pm Mon-Wed & Sat, to 8pm Thu & Fri, to 6pm Sun; 5, 21, 47, 49, M Van Ness)

Isotope COMICS

29 Map p98, B3

Toilet seats signed by famous cartoonists over the front counter show just how seriously Isotope takes comics. Newbies tentatively flip through superhero serials, while fanboys eye the latest limited-edition graphic novels and head upstairs to lounge with local cartoonists – some of whom teach comics classes here. Don't miss signings and epic over-21 launch parties. (415-621-6543; www.isotopecomics.com; 326 Fell St; 11am-7pm Tue-Fri, to 6pm Sat & Sun; ; 5, 21, 47, 49)

Explore

The Mission

San Francisco's original neighborhood was built around an 18th-century Spanish mission where nothing seemed to grow, until the Gold Rush brought boatloads of adventurers, and wild speculation took root. The Mission remains fertile ground for vivid imaginations and tall tales told over strong drink – hence mural-lined streets, pirate supplies and literary bar crawls.

The Sights in a Day

Walk mural-covered, bookstore-lined 24th St to **Balmy Alley** (p116), where the 1970s Mission muralist movement began. Fuel up with a caffeinated beverage at **Ritual Coffee Roasters** (p122), followed by window-shopping along Valencia St, where you can browse pirate supplies and watch ichthyoid antics in the fish theater at **826 Valencia** (p116).

Sample the thin-crust delicacies at **Pizzeria Delfina** (p119) on your way to local nonprofit **Creativity Explored** (p116), featuring colorful artwork by developmentally disabled artists. Afterwards, duck into San Francisco's first building, the Spanish adobe **Mission Dolores** (p117), and pay your respects at the memorial to its native Ohlone and Miwok builders in the adjacent cemetery. Afterwards, find your new favorite flavor of ice cream at **Humphry Slocombe.** (p119)

Continue your artistic exploration at **Galería de la Raza** (p116) before burritos at **Pancho Villa** (p118). Catch an indie movie at the **Roxie Cinema** (p124), then discuss over speakeasy cocktails at **Dalva & Hideout** (p121).

For a local's day in The Mission, see p112.

Local Life

Sunny Mission Stroll (p112)

Best of San Francisco

Shopping

Little Paper Planes (p125)

Heath Ceramics (p126)

Drinks

Dalva & Hideout (p121)

%ABV (p120)

Elixir (p121)

Entertainment

Roxie Cinema (p124)

Oberlin Dance Collective (p124)

Getting There

B **BART** Stations at 16th and 24th Sts.

Bus Bus 14 runs through SoMa to the Mission; 33 links to the Castro; 22 connects to the Haight.

M **Streetcar** The J Church heads from downtown past Dolores Park.

Local Life
Sunny Mission Stroll

No matter how foggy it gets in Golden Gate Park, San Francisco's mysterious micro-climates keep most afternoons sunny in the Mission. Join sun-worship in progress year-round in Dolores Park, line up behind velvet ropes for Bi-Rite ice cream, glimpse what's growing in Dearborn Community Garden and getting graffitied on Clarion Alley, and call it an early happy hour/late lunch at Mission Cheese.

1 Watch Graffiti in Clarion Alley

Most graffiti artists shun broad daylight – but not in **Clarion Alley** (btwn 17th & 18th Sts; 14, 22, 33, B 16th St Mission, M J), SF's street-art showcase. On sunny days and with prior consent of Clarion Alley Collective, local street artists paint new murals and touch up tagged works. A few pieces survive for years, such as Megan Wilson's daisy-covered *Tax the Rich* or Jet Martinez'

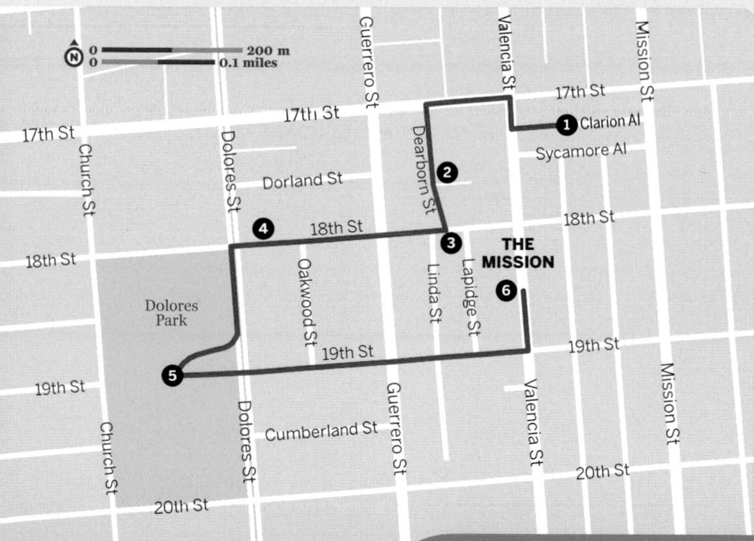

glimpse of Clarion Alley inside a man standing in a forest.

2 Sniff Roses in Dearborn Community Garden

Flowers push through sidewalks elsewhere, but in the Mission, a rogue garden has taken over an entire parking lot. PepsiCo employees once parked on asphalt along Dearborn St, just north of 18th St and west of Valencia St. Neighbors gardened along the edges, but when the Pepsi plant closed in 1991, they got organized. Vegetable plots were planted, property taxes paid and benches installed. Today the garden feeds 40 families, and pleases passersby.

3 Glimpse Goddesses in Women's Building Murals

The nation's first women-owned-and-operated community center has quietly done good work with 170 women's organizations since 1979, but the 1994 *Maestrapeace* mural showed the **Women's Building** (415-431-1180; www.womensbuilding.org; 3543 18th St; ; 14, 22, 33, 49, B 16th St Mission, M J) for the landmark it truly is. Seven *muralistas* (muralists) and dozens of volunteers covered the building with goddesses and women trailblazers, including Nobel Prize–winner Rigoberta Menchu, poet Audre Lorde and artist Georgia O'Keeffe.

4 Indulge at Bi-Rite Creamery

Velvet ropes at clubs seem pretentious in laid-back San Francisco, but at organic **Bi-Rite Creamery** (415-626-5600; www.biritecreamery.com; 3692 18th St; ice cream $3.50-8; 11am-10pm; ; 33, B 16th St Mission, M J) they make perfect sense. The line wraps around the corner for salted-caramel ice cream with housemade hot fudge, or Sonoma honey-lavender ice cream packed into waffle cones. For a quicker fix, get balsamic strawberry soft serve at the window (1pm to 9pm).

5 Dawdle in Dolores Park

The Mission's living room is **Dolores Park** (http://sfrecpark.org/destination/mission-dolores-park; Dolores St, btwn 18th & 20th Sts; 6am-10pm; ; 14, 33, 49, B 16th St Mission, M J), site of semiprofessional tanning, free shows and Mayan-pyramid playground (sorry kids: no blood sacrifice allowed). Join serious soccer games and lazy Frisbee sessions on flat patches; tennis and basketball courts are open to anyone who's got game. Don't miss downtown panoramas from hillside benches.

6 Mellow Out at Mission Cheese

Wrought-iron dancing skeletons embedded in Valencia St sidewalks mark your path to **Mission Cheese** (415-553-8667; www.missioncheese.net; 736 Valencia St; 11am-9pm Tue-Thu & Sun, to 10pm Fri & Sat; ; 14, 22, 33, 49, J, B 16th St Mission). Place your order at the counter, then grab sidewalk seating to gloat over creamy California goat's cheeses, sip Sonoma wines and trend-spot Mission street fashion.

400 m
0.2 miles
0
0
N
A
B
C
D
E
1
2
3
4
Franklin Square
York St
Bryant St
Florida St
Alabama St
Harrison St
Treat Ave
Folsom St
Shotwell St
S Van Ness Ave
Capp St
Natoma St
Minna St
Otis St
Erie St
Central Fwy
14th St
15th St
16th St
17th St
18th St
19th St
Mariposa St
Adair St
16th St Mission
Hoff St
Rondel Pl
Clarion Al
San Carlos St
Lexington St
Valencia St
Lapidge St
Dearborn St
Albion St
Duboce Ave
Clinton Park
Brosnan St
Guerrero St
Market St
Dolores St
Dorland St
Oakwood St
Creativity Explored
Mission Dolores
4
5
8
10
13
17
18
19
22
24
25
27
31
32
33
34

THE MISSION

NOE VALLEY

Dolores Park

Garfield Square

20th St
21st St
22nd St
23rd St
24th St
25th St
26th St
Bryant St
Florida St
Alabama St
Harrison St
Treat Ave
Lucky St
Folsom St
Horace St
Shotwell St
Virgil St
S Van Ness Ave
Cypress St
Capp St
Lilac St
Mission St
Osage St
Bartlett St
Orange Al
Valencia St
Poplar St
San Jose Ave
Hill St
Alvarado St
Elizabeth St
Guerrero St
Ames St
Fair Oaks St
Quane St
Dolores St
Chattanooga St
Cumberland St
Liberty St

1 826 Valencia
2 Balmy Alley
3 Precita Eyes Mission Mural Tours
24th St Mission

A B C D E
5 6 7 8

For reviews see

Sights p116
Eating p118
Drinking p120
Entertainment p123
Shopping p125

Sights

826 Valencia

CULTURAL CENTER

1 Map p114, B5

Avast, ye scurvy scalawags! If ye be shipwrecked without yer eye patch or McSweeney's literary anthology, lay down ye doubloons and claim yer booty at this here nonprofit Pirate Store. Below decks, kids be writing tall tales for dark nights a'sea, and ye can study writing movies and science fiction and suchlike, if that be yer dastardly inclination. Arrrr! (415-642-5905; www.826valencia.org; 826 Valencia St; noon-6pm; ; 14, 33, 49, B 16th St Mission, M J)

> Local Life
>
> **Galería de la Raza**
>
> Art never forgets its roots at this nonprofit that has showcased Latino art since 1970. Culture and community are constantly being redefined at **Galería de la Raza** (Map p114, E7; 415-826-8009; www.galeriadelaraza.org; 2857 24th St; donations welcome; during exhibitions noon-6pm Wed-Sat; ; 10, 14, 33, 48, 49, B 24th St Mission), from contemporary Mexican photography and group shows exploring Latin gay culture to performances capturing community responses to Mission gentrification.

Balmy Alley

PUBLIC ART

2 Map p114, D7

Inspired by Diego Rivera's 1930s San Francisco murals and provoked by US foreign policy in Central America, 1970s Mission *muralistas* (muralists) led by Mia Gonzalez set out to transform the political landscape, one mural-covered garage door at a time. Today, Balmy Alley murals span three decades, from an early memorial for El Salvador activist Archbishop Óscar Romero to a homage to Frida Kahlo, Georgia O'Keeffe and other trailblazing women modern artists. (415-285-2287; www.precitaeyes.org; btwn 24th & 25th Sts; 10, 12, 14, 27, 48, B 24th St Mission)

Precita Eyes Mission Mural Tours

WALKING

3 Map p114, E7

Muralists lead weekend walking tours covering 60 to 70 Mission murals within a six- to 10-block radius of mural-bedecked Balmy Alley (p116). Tours last 90 minutes to two hours and 15 minutes (for the more in-depth Classic Mural Walk). Proceeds fund mural upkeep at this community arts nonprofit. (415-285-2287; www.precitaeyes.org; 2981 24th St; adult $15-20, child $3; ; 12, 14, 48, 49, B 24th St Mission)

Creativity Explored

GALLERY

4 Map p114, A3

Brave new worlds are captured in celebrated artworks destined for museum retrospectives, international

NAGEL PHOTOGRAPHY/SHUTTERSTOCK ©

Mission Dolores

shows, and even Marc Jacobs handbags and CB2 pillowcases – all by the local developmentally disabled artists who create at this nonprofit center. Intriguing themes range from monsters to Morse code, and openings are joyous celebrations with the artists, their families and rock-star fan base. (☎415-863-2108; www.creativityexplored.org; 3245 16th St; donations welcome; ⊙10am-3pm Mon-Wed & Fri, to 7pm Thu, noon-5pm Sat & Sun; 👪; 🚌14, 22, 33, 49, B 16th St Mission, M J)

Mission Dolores

CHURCH

5 👁 Map p114, A3

The city's oldest building and its namesake, whitewashed adobe Misión San Francisco de Asís was founded in 1776 and rebuilt from 1782 with conscripted Ohlone and Miwok labor – a graveyard memorial hut commemorates 5000 Ohlone and Miwok laborers who died in mission measles epidemics in the early 19th century. Today the modest adobe structure is overshadowed by the ornate adjoining 1913 basilica, featuring stained-glass windows depicting California's 21 missions. (Misión San Francisco de Asís; ☎415-621-8203; www.missiondolores.org; 3321 16th St; adult/child $5/3; ⊙9am-4pm Nov-Apr, to 4:30pm May-Oct; 🚌22, 33, B 16th St Mission, M J)

Eating

Al's Place

CALIFORNIAN $$

6 Map p114, B8

The Golden State dazzles on Al's plates, featuring homegrown heirloom ingredients, pristine Pacific seafood, and grass-fed meat on the side. Painstaking preparation yields sun-drenched flavors and exquisite textures: crispy-skin cod with frothy preserved-lime dip, grilled peach melting into velvety foie gras. Dishes are half the size but thrice the flavor of mains elsewhere – get two or three, and you'll be California dreaming. (415-416-6136; www.alsplacesf.com; 1499 Valencia St; share plates $15-19; 5:30-10pm Wed-Sun; ; 12, 14, 49, M J, B 24th St Mission)

Top Tip

Top Five Mission Tacos

La Palma Mexicatessen (Map p114, E7; 415-647-1500; www.lapalmasf.com; 2884 24th St; tamales, tacos & huarache $3-5; 8am-6pm Mon-Sat, to 5pm Sun; ; 12, 14, 27, 48, B 24th St Mission)

Pancho Villa (Map p114, B3; 415-864-8840; www.sfpanchovilla.com; 3071 16th St; burritos $5-10; 10am-midnight; ; 14, 22, 33, 49, B 16th St Mission)

Namu Gaji (Map p114, A4; 415-431-6268; www.namusf.com; 499 Dolores St; share plates $10-19; 5:30-10pm Tue, 11:30am-3pm & 5:30-10pm Wed-Fri, 10:30am-4pm & 5-10pm Sat & Sun; 14, 22, 33, 49, M J, B 16th St Mission)

Tacolicious (Map p114, B5; 415-649-6077; http://tacolicious.com; 741 Valencia St; tacos $4; 11:30am-midnight; ; 14, 22, 33, 49, B 16th St Mission, M J)

La Taqueria (above, right)

La Taqueria

MEXICAN $

7 Map p114

SF's definitive burrito has no saffron rice, spinach tortilla or mango salsa – just perfectly grilled meats, slow-cooked beans and tomatillo or mesquite salsa wrapped in a flour tortilla. They're purists at James Beard Award–winning La Taqueria – you'll pay extra to go without beans, because they add more meat – but spicy pickles and *crema* (sour cream) bring burrito bliss. Worth the wait, always. (415-285-7117; 2889 Mission St; items $3-11; 11am-9pm Mon-Sat, to 8pm Sun; ; 12, 14, 48, 49, B 24th St Mission)

Craftsman & Wolves

BAKERY, CALIFORNIAN $

8 Map p114, B4

Breakfast routines are made to be broken by the infamous Rebel Within: a sausage-spiked Asiago-cheese muffin with a silken soft-boiled egg baked inside. SF's surest pick-me-up is a Highwire macchiato with matcha (green tea) cookies; a Thai coconut-curry scone enjoyed with pea soup and rosé is lunch perfected. Exquisite hazelnut cube-cakes and vanilla-violet

cheesecakes are ideal for celebrating unbirthdays and imaginary holidays. (415-913-7713; http://craftsman-wolves.com; 746 Valencia St; pastries $3-8; 7am-6pm Mon-Fri, from 8am Sat & Sun; 14, 22, 33, 49, B 16th St Mission, M J)

Ichi Sushi

SUSHI $$

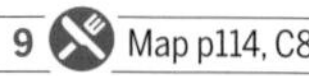

Alluring on the plate and positively obscene on the tongue, Ichi Sushi is a sharp cut above other seafood joints. Chef Tim Archuleta slices silky, sustainably sourced fish with a jeweler's precision, balances it atop well-packed rice, and tops it with tiny but powerfully tangy dabs of gelled *yuzu* and microscopically cut spring onion and chili daikon that make soy sauce unthinkable. (415-525-4750; www.ichisushi.com; 3369 Mission St; sushi $4-8; 11:30am-2pm & 5:30-10pm Mon-Thu, to 11pm Fri & Sat, 5:30-9:30pm Sun; 14, 24, 49, B 24th St Mission, M J)

Pizzeria Delfina

PIZZA $$

One bite explains why SF is obsessed with pizza lately: Delfina's thin crust heroically supports the weight of fennel sausage and fresh mozzarella without drooping or cracking. On sauce-free white pizzas, chefs freestyle with California ingredients such as broccoli rabe, Maitake mushrooms and artisan cheese. No reservations; sign the chalkboard and wait with a glass of wine at next-door Delfina bar. (415-437-6800; www.delfinasf.com; 3621 18th St; pizzas $14-19; 5-10pm Tue, 11:30am-10pm Mon, Wed & Thu, to 11pm Fri, noon-11pm Sat, to 10pm Sun; 14, 22, 33, 49, M J, B 16th St Mission)

Local Life

Cooking in the Mission

Inspired by Mission cuisine? Hands-on, low-cost cooking and knife-skills classes, artisan cheese and wine tastings, and even edible perfume workshops are available at nonprofit **18 Reasons** (Map p114, B4; 415-568-2710; www.18reasons.org; 3674 18th St; classes & dining events $12-125; ; 22, 33, M J). Spots fill quickly, so book early. Mingle with fellow foodies at $10 Wednesday community suppers and $3 to $10 Thursday happy hours.

Humphry Slocombe

ICE CREAM $

11 Map p114, D7

Indie-rock organic ice cream may permanently spoil you for Top 40 flavors. Once 'Elvis: The Fat Years' (banana and peanut butter) and Hibiscus Beet Sorbet have rocked your taste buds, cookie dough seems so basic – and ordinary sundaes can't compare to 'Secret Breakfast' (bourbon and cornflakes) and Blue Bottle Vietnamese Coffee drizzled with hot fudge, California olive oil and sea salt. (415-550-6971; www.humphryslocombe.com; 2790 Harrison St; ice creams $4-6; 1-11pm Mon-Fri, from noon Sat & Sun; ; 12, 14, 49, B 24th St Mission)

Udupi Palace
SOUTH INDIAN $

12 Map p114, B6

Tandoori in the Tenderloin is for novices – SF foodies queue for the bright, clean flavors of Udupi's South Indian *dosa* (light, crispy lentil-flour pancake) dipped in *sambar* (vegetable stew) and coconut chutney. Marathoners may need help finishing the 2ft-long paper *dosa* – save room for pea-and-onion *uthappam* (lentil-flour pancake) and *bagala bhath* (yogurt rice with nutty toasted mustard seeds). (415-970-8000; www.udupipalaceca.com; 1007 Valencia St; mains $8-12; 11:30am-10pm Sun-Thu, to 10:30pm Fri & Sat; ; 12, 14, 33, 49, B 24th St Mission)

Drinking

%ABV
COCKTAIL BAR

13 Map p114, B3

As kindred spirits will deduce from the name (the abbreviation for 'percent alcohol by volume'), this bar is backed by cocktail crafters who know their Rittenhouse rye from their Japanese malt whisky. Top-notch hooch is served promptly and without pretension, including excellent Cali wine and beer on tap and original historically inspired cocktails like the Sutro Swizzle (Armagnac, grapefruit shrub, maraschino liqueur). (415-400-4748; www.abvsf.com; 3174 16th St; 2pm-2am; 14, 22, B 16th St Mission, M J)

Trick Dog
BAR

14 Map p114, E5

Drink adventurously with ingenious cocktails inspired by local obsessions: San Francisco muralists, Chinese diners or conspiracy theories. Every six months, Trick Dog adopts a new theme and the entire menu changes – proof that you can teach an old dog new tricks, and improve on classics like the Manhattan. Arrive early for bar stools or hit the mood-lit loft for high-concept bar bites. (415-471-2999; www.trickdogbar.com; 3010 20th St; 3pm-2am; 12, 14, 49)

El Rio
CLUB

15 Map p114, C8

Work it all out on the dance floor with SF's most down and funky crowd – the full rainbow spectrum of colorful characters is here to party. Calendar highlights include Salsa Sunday, free oysters from 5:30pm Friday, drag-star DJs, backyard bands and ping-pong. Expect knockout margaritas and shameless flirting on a patio that's seen it all since 1978. Cash only. (415-282-3325; www.elriosf.com; 3158 Mission St; cover free-$8; 1pm-2am; 12, 14, 27, 49, B 24th St Mission)

20 Spot
WINE BAR

16  Map p114, C5

Find your California mellow at this neighborhood wine lounge in a 1895 Victorian building. After decades as Force of Habit punk-record shop –

La Taqueria (p118)

note the vintage sign – this corner joint has earned the right to unwind with a glass of Berkeley's Donkey and Goat sparkling wine and not get any guff. Caution: oysters with pickled persimmon could become a habit. (☎415-624-3140; www.20spot.com; 3565 20th St; ⏰5pm-midnight Mon-Thu, to 1am Fri & Sat; 🚌14, 22, 33, **B** 16th St Mission)

Dalva & Hideout

LOUNGE

17 Map p114, B3

SF's best bars are distinguished not just by their drinks but by the conversations they inspire – and by both measures Dalva is top shelf. Here Roxie (p124) movie critiques drip with Irony Pinot Noir, politics invoke Russian River Damnation ale, and Dolores Park gossip spills over Dirty Pigeons (mezcal, lime, grapefruit, gentian-flower bitters) at back-room Hideout (from 7pm; cash only). (☎415-252-7740; http://dalvasf.com; 3121 16th St; ⏰4pm-2am; 🚌14, 22, 33, 49, **B** 24th St Mission)

Elixir

BAR

18 Map p114, B3

Do the planet a favor and have another drink at SF's first certified green bar, in an actual 1858 Wild West saloon. Elixir expertly blends farm-fresh seasonal mixers with local small-batch, organic, biodynamic spirits – Meyer-lemon and rye sours

JOHN S LANDER/GETTY IMAGES ©

Roxie Cinema (p124)

and Mission Pimm's Cup with pisco and cucumber vodka get everyone air-guitar rocking to the killer jukebox. Proceeds from drink-for-a-cause Wednesdays support local charities. (☎415-522-1633; www.elixirsf.com; 3200 16th St; ⏰3pm-2am Mon-Fri, from noon Sat, from 10am Sun; 🚌14, 22, 33, 49, B 16th St Mission, M J)

Zeitgeist

BAR

19 Map p114, B1

You've got two seconds flat to order from tough-gal barkeeps used to putting macho bikers in their place – but with 48 beers on draft, you're spoiled for choice. Epic afternoons unfold in the graveled beer garden, with folks hanging out and smoking at long picnic tables. SF's longest happy hour lasts 9am to 8pm weekdays. Cash only; no photos (read: no evidence). (☎415-255-7505; www.zeitgeistsf.com; 199 Valencia St; ⏰9am-2am; 🚌14, 22, 49, B 16th St Mission)

Ritual Coffee Roasters

CAFE

20 Map p114, B6

Cults wish they inspired the same devotion as Ritual, where regulars solemnly queue for house-roasted cappuccino with ferns drawn in foam and specialty drip coffees with highly distinctive flavor profiles – descriptions comparing roasts to grapefruit peel or hazelnut aren't exaggerating. Electrical outlets are limited to encourage conversation, so you can eavesdrop on dates and political-protest plans. (☎415-641-1011; www.ritualroasters.com; 1026 Valencia St; ⏰6am-8pm Mon-Sat, from 7am Sat & Sun; 🚌14, 49, B 24th St Mission)

Borderlands

CAFE

21 Map p114, B5

West Coast coffeehouse culture is staging a comeback at this membership-supported neighborhood bookstore-cafe, complete with hairless cats, creaky wooden floors, top-notch hot chocolate and sofas encouraging offline chats. Mysterious yet sociable Borderlands limits wi-fi (9am to 5pm weekdays) to keep conversation flowing and thoughtfully provides racks of paperback mysteries for browsing – or buying at the 1950s

purchase price of 50¢. Cash only. (☎415-970-6998; www.borderlands-cafe.com; 870 Valencia St; ⊙8am-8pm; 🚌14, 33, 49, B16th St Mission)

Bissap Baobab

CLUB

22 Map p114, C4

A Senegalese restaurant early in the evening, Baobab brings on the DJ or live act around 10pm – and before you can say 'tamarind margarita,' tables are shoved out of the way to make room on the dance floor. Mid-week Cuban timba salsa, occasional flamenco and gypsy jazz shows, and Friday and Saturday Paris-Dakar Afrobeat get the Mission in a universal groove. (☎415-826-9287; www.bissapbaobab.com; 3372 19th St; cover free-$5; ⊙club 9pm or 10pm-2am Thu-Sat; 🚌14, 22, 33, 49, B16th St Mission)

Entertainment

Alamo Drafthouse Cinema

CINEMA

23 Map p114, C6

The landmark 1932 New Mission cinema, now restored to its original Timothy Pfleuger–designed art-deco glory, has a new mission: to upgrade dinner-and-a-movie dates. Staff deliver microbrews and tasty fare to plush banquette seats, so you don't miss a moment of the premieres, cult revivals (especially Music Mondays) or SF favorites from *Mrs Doubtfire* to *Dirty Harry* – often with filmmaker Q&As. (☎415-549-5959; https://drafthouse.com/sf; 2550 Mission St; tickets $9-20; 👪; 🚌14, B24th St Mission)

Chapel

LIVE MUSIC

24 Map p114, B4

Musical prayers are answered in a 1914 California Craftsman landmark with heavenly acoustics. The 40ft roof is regularly raised by shows by New Orleans brass bands, folkYEAH! Americana groups, legendary rockers like Peter Murphy and hip-hop icons such as Prince Paul. Many shows are all ages, except when comedians like W Kamau Bell test edgy material. (☎415-551-5157; www.thechapelsf.com; 777 Valencia St; cover $15-40; ⊙bar 7pm-2am; 🚌14, 33, MJ, B16th St Mission)

Mission Street Smarts

Bars and restaurants make Mission a key nightlife destination, but it's not always the safest area to walk alone at night. Recruit a friend and be alert in the Mission east of Valencia, especially around 19th St gang-turf boundaries. Don't bring the bling – this isn't LA – or dawdle around BART stations. You should be fine in the daytime, but don't leave items like laptops and phones unattended at cafes.

Oberlin Dance Collective DANCE

25 Map p114, C3

For 45 years, ODC has been redefining dance with risky, raw performances and the sheer joy of movement. ODC's season runs September to December, but its stage presents year-round shows featuring local and international artists. ODC Dance Commons is a hub and hangout for the dance community offering 200-plus classes a week, from flamenco to vogue; all ages and skill levels welcome. (ODC; box office 415-863-9834, classes 415-549-8519; www.odctheater.org; 3153 17th St; drop-in classes from $15, shows $20-50; 12, 14, 22, 33, 49, B 16th St Mission)

Brava Theater THEATER

26 Map p114, E7

Brava's been producing women-run theater for 30-plus years, hosting acts from comedian Sandra Bernhard to V-day monologist Eve Ensler, and it's the nation's first company with a commitment to producing original works by women of color and LGBT playwrights. Brava honors the Mission's Mexican heritage with Latinx music and dance celebrations, plus hand-painted show posters modeled after Mexican cinema billboards. (415-641-7657; www.brava.org; 2781 24th St; ; 12, 27, 33, 48)

Roxie Cinema CINEMA

27 Map p114, B3

This vintage 1909 cinema is a neighborhood nonprofit with an international reputation for distributing documentaries and showing controversial films banned elsewhere. Tickets to film-festival premieres, rare revivals and raucous Oscars telecasts sell out – get tickets online – but if the main show's packed, discover riveting documentaries in teensy next-door Little Roxy instead. No ads, plus personal introductions to every film. (415-863-1087; www.roxie.com; 3117 16th St; regular screening/matinee $11/8; 14, 22, 33, 49, B 16th St Mission)

Marsh THEATER, COMEDY

28 Map p114, B6

Choose your seat wisely: you may spend the evening on the edge of it. One-acts and monologues here involve the audience in the creative process, from comedian W Kamau Bell's riffs to live tapings of National Public Radio's *Philosophy Talk*. Sliding-scale pricing allows everyone to participate, and a few reserved seats are sometimes available (tickets $55). (415-282-3055; www.themarsh.org; 1062 Valencia St; tickets $15-35; box office 1-4pm Mon-Fri; 12, 14, 48, 49, B 24th St Mission)

JEJIM/GETTY IMAGES ©

Dolores Park (p113)

Amnesia

LIVE MUSIC

29 Map p114, B5

Forget standard playlists – this closet-sized boho dive will make you lose your mind for Monday bluegrass jams, Tuesday Troubled Comedy sessions, Wednesday gaucho jazz, random readings and breakout dance parties. Shows are cheap and often sliding scale, so the crowd is pumped and the beer flows freely. Check Facebook or just go with the flow; $5 craft beer from 4pm to 7pm. (415-970-0012; www.facebook.com/amnesiaSF; 853 Valencia St; cover free-$10; 4pm-2am Mon-Fri, from noon Sat & Sun; 14, 33, 49, B 16th St Mission)

Shopping

Little Paper Planes

GIFTS & SOUVENIRS

30 Map p114, B5

Explore fresh gift possibilities at this purveyor of essential SF oddities: SF artist Kelly Lynn Jones' ocean-print scarves, Oakland-made cacti-print wallets, ecofriendly glossy black nail polish made in California and house-published manifestos (including *Art as a Muscular Principle* and *Bay Area Women Artists*). The place is tiny, but it thinks big – LPP's artists' residency yields original works like Hannah Perrine's paper-airplane prints. (415-643-4616; http://littlepaper-

Local Life

The Mission's Community-Supported Bookstore Scene

San Francisco may be the global hub for all things digital, but an analog revolution is afoot in the Mission. The district has rallied around the once-struggling **Adobe Books** (Map p114, D7; 415-864-3936; www.adobebookshop.com; 3130 24th St; noon-8pm Mon-Fri, from 11am Sat & Sun; 12, 14, 48, 49, B 24th St Mission), now reinvented as a member-supported collective hosting raucous readings and Backroom Gallery art openings with a track record of launching Whitney Biennial stars. Down 24th St from Adobe, **Alley Cat Books** (Map p114, D7; 415-824-1761; www.alleycatbookshop.com; 3036 24th St; 10am-9pm Mon-Sat, to 8pm Sun; ; 12, 14, 48, 49, B 24th St Mission) is part bookstore, part community center, with bilingual books in the front, art shows in the middle, and events and a ping-pong table in back. On Valencia St, Alley Cat's sibling bookstore **Dog-Eared Books** (Map p114, D5; 415-282-1901; www.dogearedbooks.com; 900 Valencia St; 10am-10pm; 12, 14, 33, 49) supports new releases and small presses with author readings and commemorates bygone cultural figures in hand-drawn obituaries. Further along Valencia, member-supported **Borderlands** (p122) upholds San Francisco's noir-novel reputation, selling 50¢ mysteries to read in the convivial cafe.

planes.com; 855 Valencia St; noon-7pm Mon-Sat, to 6pm Sun; 14, 33, 49, B 16th St Mission, M J)

Bi-Rite

FOOD & DRINKS

31 Map p114, A4

Diamond counters can't compare to the foodie dazzle of Bi-Rite's sublime wall of local artisan chocolates, treasure boxes of organic fruit, and California wine and cheese selections expertly curated by upbeat, knowledgeable staff. Step up to the altar-like deli counter to provision five-star Dolores Park picnics. An institution since 1940, Bi-Rite champions good food for all through its nonprofit 18 Reasons (p119). (415-241-9760; www.biritemarket.com; 3639 18th St; 8am-9pm; ; 14, 22, 33, 49, B 16th St Mission, M J)

Heath Ceramics & Newsstand

CERAMICS

32 Map p114, E4

No local, artisan SF restaurant decor is complete without earthy Heath stoneware, including the hand-glazed tiles found at this Mission studio-showroom. New Heath models are sold here alongside a design-mag newsstand, artisan pop-ups and jewelry trunk shows. Factory tours are available weekends at 11:30am; working tours are held the first and third Fridays of each month at 11:15am. (415-361-5552; www.heathceramics.com; 2900 18th St; 8am-6pm Sun-Wed, to 7pm Thu-Sat; 12, 22, 27, 33)

Generator Mural, by artists Aaron Noble & Andrew Schoultz

Aggregate Supply

CLOTHING, HOMEWARES

33 Map p114, B4

Wild West modern is the look at Aggregate Supply, purveyors of California-cool fashion and home decor. Local designers and indie makers get pride of place, including vintage Heath stoneware mugs, Turk+Taylor's plaid shirt-jackets, and SF artist Tauba Auerbach's 24-hour clocks. Souvenirs don't get more authentically local than Aggregate Supply's own op-art California graphic tee and NorCal-forest-scented organic soaps. (415-474-3190; www.AggregateSupplySF.com; 806 Valencia St; 11am-7pm Mon-Sat, noon-6pm Sun; 14, 33, 49, B 16th St Mission)

Nooworks

CLOTHING

34 Map p114, B2

Get a streetwise Mission edge with Nooworks' locally designed, US-made fashions, most under $100. Nooworks' open-mouth shirts are ideal for Pancho-Villa-burrito-and-Roxie-documentary dates, and 'Muscle Beach' maxi dresses are Dolores Park ready with psychedelic rainbows and Schwarzenegger-esque flexing bodybuilders. Kids are good to go to any Mission gallery opening in soft leggings and tees in feather-, forest- and desert-inspired graphic prints. (415-829-7623; www.nooworks.com; 395 Valencia St; 11am-7pm Tue-Sat, to 5pm Sun & Mon; 14, 22, 33, 49, B 16th St Mission)

Local Life
The History-Making Castro

Within a few years of moving into this quaint Victorian neighborhood in the 1970s, the Castro's out-and-proud community elected Harvey Milk as the nation's first gay official. When AIDS hit, the Castro wiped its tears and got to work, advocating interventions that saved lives worldwide. Today the little neighborhood under the giant rainbow flag is a global symbol of freedom; come out and see for yourself.

Getting There

The Castro is a couple of blocks west of the Mission between 15th and 18th Sts.

Ⓜ **Streetcar** Take the scenic above-ground F line from downtown, or underground K, L and M lines.

Bus Line 33 connects to the Upper Haight and Mission; 24 runs up Divisadero St to the Haight.

❶ Come Out in Harvey Milk Plaza

A huge, irrepressibly cheerful rainbow flag waves hello as you emerge from the Castro St Muni station into **Harvey Milk Plaza**. Notice the plaque honoring the Castro camera-store-owner turned politician. He was assassinated not long after becoming America's first out gay official, but he's a living symbol of civil rights and civic pride.

❷ Toast at Twin Peaks Tavern

A vintage neon rainbow proudly points to **Twin Peaks** (☎415-864-9470; www.twinpeakstavern.com; 401 Castro St; ⊙noon-2am Mon-Fri, from 8am Sat & Sun; Ⓜ Castro St), the world's first gay bar with windows open to the street. Raise a toast to freedom, watch the gay world go by, and join the inevitable sing-along whenever an '80s anthem hits the jukebox.

❸ Walk in the Steps of LGBT Giants

Watch your step on Castro St, or you might step on Virginia Woolf without even realizing it. She's one of 20 pioneering figures featured in bronze sidewalk plaques in the Castro's new **Rainbow Honor Walk** (http://rainbowhonorwalk.org; Castro St, btwn 18th & 20th Sts; Ⓜ Castro St).

❹ Cheer at Castro Theatre

At the deco-fabulous **Castro Theatre** (☎415-621-6120; www.castrotheatre.com; 429 Castro St; adult/child $11/8.50; Ⓜ Castro St), show tunes on a Wurlitzer are overtures to independent cinema, silver-screen gems and live-action drag versions of cult classics.

❺ Head Somewhere over the Rainbow

Gay pride stops traffic at Castro and 18th Sts, where crosswalks are rainbow-striped. The southeast corner is a community hub, where protesters gather petition signatures, street altars honor bygone community members and street performers do their thing, often in gold-lamé thongs.

❻ Look Back with Pride

America's first gay-history museum, **GLBT History Museum** (☎415-621-1107; www.glbthistory.org/museum; 4127 18th St; $5, 1st Wed of month free; ⊙11am-7pm Mon-Sat, noon-5pm Sun, closed Tue fall-spring; Ⓜ Castro St) captures proud moments and historic challenges: Harvey Milk's campaign literature, interviews with trailblazing bisexual author Gore Vidal, matchbooks from long-gone bathhouses and 1950s penal codes banning homosexuality.

❼ Think Ahead at Human Rights Campaign Action Center & Store

The storefront home of the **Human Rights Campaign** (http://shop.hrc.org; 575 Castro St; ⊙10am-8pm Mon-Sat, to 7pm Sun; Ⓜ Castro St) may look familiar: this was once Harvey Milk's camera shop, as featured in the Academy Award–winning biopic *Milk*. The civil rights advocacy outpost features a stunning mural, 'Equality' wedding rings, and 'Mighty Gay' tees for superheroes with the power to leap out of the closet in a single bound.

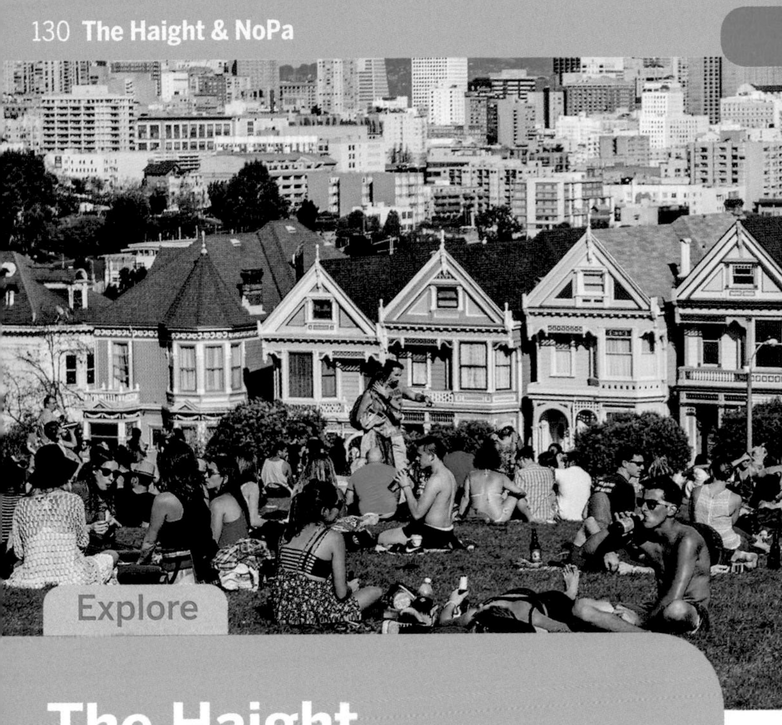

Explore

The Haight & NoPa

Was it the fall of 1966 or the winter of '67? As the Haight saying goes, if you can remember the Summer of Love, man, you probably weren't here. But it's not too late to join the revolution at radical cafes and bookstores, or make the scene at Haight and Ashbury Sts – the street corner that became the turning point of the hippie generation.

The Sights in a Day

Fuel up with baked goods at **Mill** (p135) before taking the **walking tour** (p158) to spot landmarks from the Haight's hippie heyday, including the heart of the Summer of Love: **Haight & Ashbury** (p134).

After restorative organic pub fare and a home-brew sampler at **Magnolia Brewery** (p136), shop and stroll along Haight St, making sure not to miss **Amoeba Music** (p138), **Piedmont Boutique** (p138) and **Loved to Death** (p138).

Along Divisadero St, explore NoPa (North of the Panhandle) boutiques en route to **Alamo Square Park** (p134) for breathtaking downtown views behind a jagged Victorian roofline. Hit the Lower Haight for sausages from **Rosamunde Sausage Grill** (p135) with microbrews at **Toronado** (p136) – just try not to let the 400-beer selection distract you from showtime at the **Independent** (p137).

Best of San Francisco

Drinks

Toronado (p136)

Alembic (p137)

Aub Zam Zam (p136)

Shopping

Amoeba Music (p138)

Piedmont Boutique (p138)

Wasteland (p138)

Loved to Death (p138)

Architecture

Alamo Square Park (p134)

Grateful Dead House (p134)

Eating Out

Rosamunde Sausage Grill (p135)

Live Music

Independent (p137)

Getting There

Bus Lines 6 and 7 run up Haight St; 22 links to the Mission and Marina; 24 to the Castro; 43 to the Marina; 33 to Castro and Golden Gate Park.

M Streetcar N Judah connects Upper and Lower Haight to downtown and Ocean Beach.

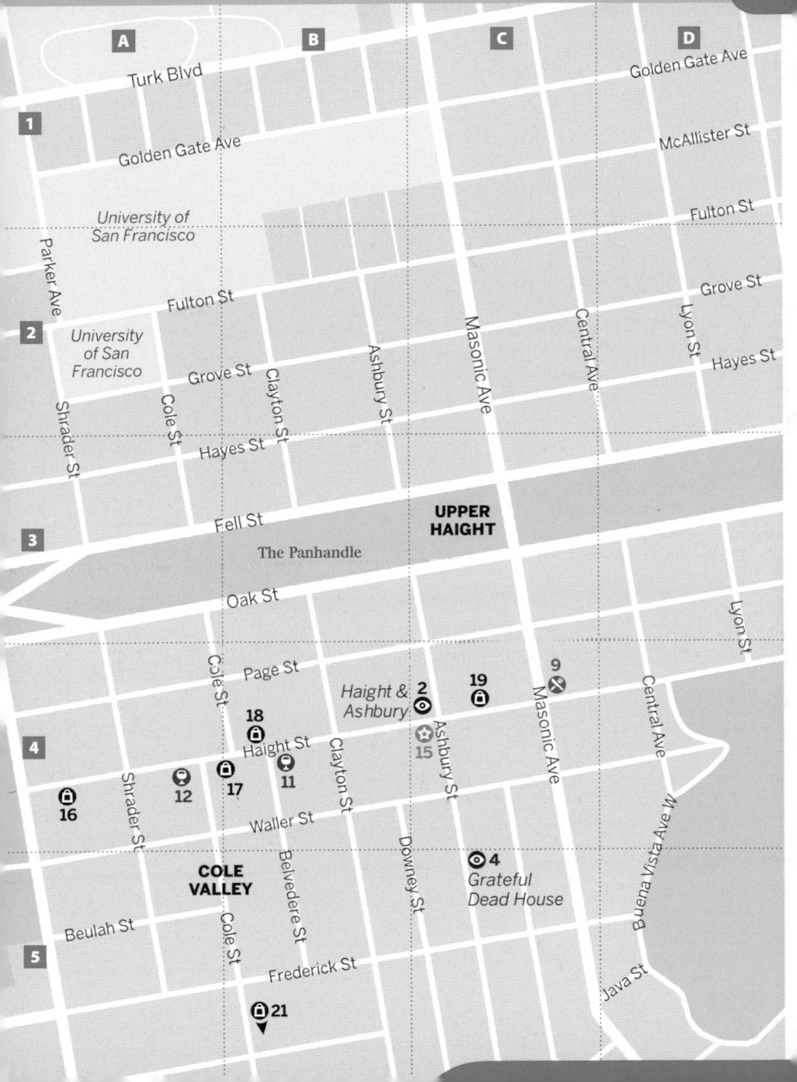

A B C D
1 2 3 4 5

Turk Blvd
Golden Gate Ave
McAllister St
Fulton St
Grove St
Hayes St
Fell St
Oak St
Page St
Haight St
Waller St
Beulah St
Frederick St
Java St
Parker Ave
Shrader St
Cole St
Clayton St
Ashbury St
Masonic Ave
Central Ave
Lyon St
Belvedere St
Downey St
Buena Vista Ave W

University of San Francisco
The Panhandle
UPPER HAIGHT
COLE VALLEY

2 Haight & Ashbury
4 Grateful Dead House
9
11
12
15
16
17
18
19
21

E
F
G
H
0
400 m
0
0.2 miles
1
2
3
4
5
Fulton St
Grove St
Hayes St
Fell St
Oak St
Page St
Haight St
Waller St
Hermann St
Duboce Ave
14th St
Henry St
15th St
Broderick St
Divisadero St
Scott St
Baker St
Pierce St
Steiner St
Fillmore St
Castro St
Alpine Tce
Buena Vista Ave E
Park Hill Ave
Noe St
Alamo Square Park
Duboce Park
Buena Vista Park
LOWER HAIGHT
For reviews see
Sights p134
Eating p135
Drinking p136
Entertainment p137
Shopping p138

Sights

Alamo Square Park

PARK

1 Map p132, G2

Hippie communes and Victorian bordellos, jazz greats and opera stars, earthquakes and Church of Satan services: these genteel 'Painted Lady' Victorian mansions have hosted them all since 1857, and survived elegantly intact. Pastel Postcard Row mansions along Alamo Sq's eastern side pale in comparison with the colorful characters along the northwestern end of this hilltop park. The northern side features Barbary Coast baroque mansions at their most bombastic, bedecked with fish-scale shingles and gingerbread trim dripping from peaked roofs. (www.sfparksalliance.org/our-parks/parks/alamo-square; cnr Hayes & Steiner Sts; sunrise-sunset; 5, 21, 22, 24)

Haight & Ashbury

LANDMARK

2 Map p132, C4

This legendary intersection was the epicenter of the psychedelic '60s, and 'Hashbury' remains a counterculture magnet. On average Saturdays here you can sign Green Party petitions, commission a poem and hear Hare Krishna on keyboards and Bob Dylan on banjo. The clock overhead always reads 4:20 – better known in herbal circles as International Bong-Hit Time. A local clockmaker recently fixed the clock; within a week it was stuck again at 4:20. (6, 7, 33, 37, 43)

Buena Vista Park

PARK

3 Map p132, E4

True to its name, this park, founded in 1867, offers splendid vistas over the city to Golden Gate Bridge. Consider them your reward for hiking up the steep hill, ringed by stately, century-old California oaks. Take Buena Vista Ave West downhill to spot Victorian mansions that survived the 1906 earthquake and fire. Note that after-hours boozing or cruising here is risky, given petty criminal activity. (http://sfrecpark.org; Haight St, btwn Central Ave & Baker St; sunrise-sunset; 6, 7, 37, 43)

Grateful Dead House

NOTABLE BUILDING

4 Map p132, C5

Like surviving members of the Grateful Dead, this purple Victorian sports a touch of gray – but, during the Summer of Love, this was where Jerry Garcia and bandmates blew minds, amps and brain cells. After their 1967 drug bust, the Dead held a press conference here arguing for decriminalization, claiming that, if everyone who smoked marijuana were arrested, San Francisco would be empty. Point taken, eventually – in 2016, California legalized adult recreational marijuana use in private (read: not this sidewalk, dude). (710 Ashbury St; 6, 7, 33, 37, 43)

Eating

Mill

BAKERY $

5 Map p132, F1

Baked with organic whole grain stone-ground on-site, hearty Josey Baker Bread sustains Haight skaters and start-uppers alike. You might think SF hipsters are gullible for queuing for pricey toast, until you taste the truth: slathered in housemade hazelnut spread or California-grown almond butter, it's a meal. Monday is pizza night, and any time's right for made-in-house granola with Sonoma yogurt. (415-345-1953; www.themillsf.com; 736 Divisadero St; toast $4-7; 7am-7pm Tue-Thu, to 8pm Fri-Sun, to 9pm Mon; ; 5, 21, 24, 38)

Brenda's Meat & Three

SOUTHERN US $

6 Map p132, E1

The name means one meaty main course plus three sides – though only superheroes finish ham steak with Creole red-eye gravy and exemplary grits, let alone cream biscuits and eggs. Chef Brenda Buenviaje's portions are defiantly Southern, which explains brunch lines of marathoners and partiers who forgot to eat last night. Arrive early, share sweet-potato pancakes, and pray for crawfish specials. (415-926-8657; http://brendasmeatandthree.com; 919 Divisadero St; mains $8-15; 8am-10pm Wed-Mon; 5, 21, 24, 38)

Local Life

Skate the Haight

Never mind the Golden Gate Bridge: for skaters, Haight St is the ultimate SF icon. The downhill slide from Buena Vista Park to the Lower Haight is captured in countless YouTube videos and SF's own *Thrasher* magazine. Gear up with Western Edition decks featuring ramshackle Victorians and get the skinny on SF street skating from skate-pro staff at **FTC Skateboarding** (Map p132, B4; 415-626-0663; www.ftcsf.com; 1632 Haight St; 11am-7pm; 6, 7, 33, 37, 43, M N). Roll to the Lower Haight for skater-designed 'Left Coast' hoodies and streetwise art openings at **Upper Playground** (Map p132, H3; 415-861-1960; www.upperplayground.com; 220 Fillmore St; 11am-7pm; 6, 7, 22, M N).

Rosamunde Sausage Grill

FAST FOOD $

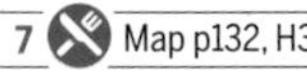
7 Map p132, H3

Impress a dinner date on the cheap: load up Coleman Farms pork Brats or free-range duck links with complimentary roasted peppers, grilled onions, whole-grain mustard and mango chutney, and enjoy with your choice of 45 seasonal draft brews at Toronado (p136) next door. To impress a local lunch date, call ahead or line up by 11:30am Tuesday for massive $6 burgers. (415-437-6851; http://rosamundesausagegrill.com; 545 Haight St;

sausages $8-8.50; ⏲11:30am-10pm Sun-Wed, to 11pm Thu-Sat; 🚌6, 7, 22, Ⓜ N)

Ragazza

PIZZA $$

8 Map p132, F3

'Girl' is what the name means, as in, 'Oooh, *girl*, did you try the wild-nettle pizza?!' Artisan *salumi* is the star of many Ragazza pizzas, from the Amatriciana with pecorino, pancetta and egg to the Moto with Calabrian chili and sausage – best with carafes of rustic Tuscan reds or Fort Point beer. Arrive early to nab garden-patio tables. (☎415-255-1133; www.ragazzasf.com; 311 Divisadero St; pizzas $14-19; ⏲5-10pm Sun-Thu, to 10:30pm Fri & Sat; 👪; 🚌6, 7, 21, 24)

Magnolia Brewery

CALIFORNIAN $$

9 Map p132, C4

Organic pub grub and home-brew samplers keep conversation flowing at communal tables, while grass-fed burgers satisfy stoner appetites in booths – it's like the Summer of Love all over again, only with better food. Morning-after brunches of housemade sausage-and-egg sandwiches and Thursday-night fried chicken are plenty curative, but Cole Porter pints are powerful enough to revive the Grateful Dead. (☎415-864-7468; www.magnoliapub.com; 1398 Haight St; mains $14-26; ⏲11am-11pm Mon-Thu, to midnight Fri, 10am-midnight Sat, to 11pm Sun; 🚌6, 7, 33, 43)

Drinking

Toronado

PUB

10 Map p132, H3

Glory hallelujah, beer-lovers: your prayers are answered. Genuflect before the chalkboard altar that lists 40-plus beers on tap and hundreds more bottled, including sensational seasonal microbrews. Bring cash for all-day happy hours and score sausages from Rosamunde (p135) to accompany ale made by Trappist monks. It sometimes gets too loud to hear your date talk, but you'll hear angels sing. (☎415-863-2276; www.toronado.com; 547 Haight St; ⏲11:30am-2am; 🚌6, 7, 22, Ⓜ N)

Aub Zam Zam

BAR

11 Map p132, B4

Persian arches, *One Thousand and One Nights* murals, 1930s jazz on the jukebox and top-shelf cocktails at low-shelf prices have brought Bohemian bliss to Haight St since 1941. Legendary founder Bruno used to throw people out for ordering a vodka martini, but he was a softie in the end, bequeathing his beloved bar to regulars who had become friends. Cash only. (☎415-861-2545; 1633 Haight St; ⏲3pm-2am Mon-Fri, 1pm-2am Sat & Sun; 🚌6, 7, 22, 33, 43, Ⓜ N)

Alembic

BAR

12 Map p132, A4

The tin ceilings are hammered and the floors well stomped, but drinks expertly crafted from 250 specialty spirits aren't made for pounding – hence the 'No Red Bull/No Jägermeister' sign and the dainty duck-heart bar snacks. 'Blood In, Blood Out' cocktails (rye, blood-orange shrub, egg white) prompt eternal Haight debates (Janis or Jimi?), but everyone loves the Sourdough (rum, grapefruit bitters, sourdough). (415-666-0822; www.alembicbar.com; 1725 Haight St; 4pm-midnight Mon & Tue, to 2am Wed-Fri, 2pm-2am Sat, 2pm-midnight Sun; 6, 7, 33, 37, 43, M N)

Madrone Art Bar

BAR

13 Map p132, F2

Drinking becomes an art form at this Victorian parlor crammed with graffiti installations and absinthe fountains. Motown Mondays feature the Ike Turner drink special – Hennessy served with a slap – but nothing beats Purple Thriller mash-ups at the monthly Prince-vs-Michael-Jackson throwdown. Performers redefine genres: punk-grass (bluegrass and punk), blunt-funk (reggae and soul) and church, no chaser (Sunday-morning jazz organ). Cash only. (415-241-0202; www.madroneartbar.com; 500 Divisadero St; cover free-$5; 4pm-2am Tue-Sat, 3pm-1:30am Sun; 5, 6, 7, 21, 24)

Entertainment

Independent

LIVE MUSIC

14 Map p132, F2

Bragging rights are earned with breakthrough shows at the small but mighty Independent, featuring indie dreamers (Magnetic Fields, Death Cab for Cutie), music legends (Steel Pulse, Guided by Voices), alt-pop (the Killers, Imagine Dragons) and international bands (Tokyo Chaotic, Australia's Airbourne). Ventilation is poor in this max-capacity-800 venue, but the sound is stellar, drinks reasonable and bathrooms improbably clean. (415-771-1421; www.theindependentsf.com; 628 Divisadero St; tickets $12-45; box office 11am-6pm Mon-Fri, to 9:30pm show nights; 5, 6, 7, 21, 24)

Club Deluxe

JAZZ

15  Map p132, C4

Blame it on the bossa nova or the Deluxe Spa Collins (gin, cucumber, ginger, mint, lemon and soda) – you'll be swinging before the night is through. Nightly jazz combos bring the zoot suits and lindy-hoppers to the dance floor. Expect mood lighting, cats who wear hats well and dames who can swill highballs without losing their matte red lipstick. (415-552-6949; www.clubdeluxe.co; 1511 Haight St; cover free-$10; 4pm-2am Mon-Fri, 3pm-2am Sat & Sun; 6, 7, 33, 37, 43)

Shopping

Amoeba Music

MUSIC

16 Map p132, A4

Enticements are hardly necessary to lure the masses to the West Coast's most eclectic collection of new and used music and video, but Amoeba offers listening stations, free zines with uncannily accurate staff reviews, and a free concert series that recently starred the Violent Femmes, Kehlani, Billy Bragg and Mike Doughty – plus a foundation that's saved one million acres of rainforest. (415-831-1200; www.amoeba.com; 1855 Haight St; 11am-8pm; 6, 7, 33, 43, MN)

Wasteland

VINTAGE, CLOTHING

18 Map p132, B4

Take center stage in this converted-cinema vintage superstore in barely worn Marc Jacobs frocks, vintage concert tees and a steady supply of platform go-go boots. Hip occasionally verges on hideous with sequined sweaters and '80s power suits, but, at reasonable (not bargain) prices, anyone can afford fashion risks. If you've got excess baggage, Wasteland buys clothes noon to 6pm daily. (415-863-3150; www.shopwasteland.com; 1660 Haight St; 11am-8pm Mon-Sat, noon-7pm Sun; 6, 7, 33, 37, 43, MN)

Loved to Death

GIFTS & SOUVENIRS

17 Map p132, B4

Stuffed deer exchange glassy stares with caged baby dolls over rusty dental tools: the signs are ominous, and for sale. Head upstairs for Goth gifts, including Victorian hair lockets and portable last-rites kits. Not for the faint of heart, vegans or shutterbugs – no photos allowed, though you might recognize staff from the Science Channel's *Oddities: San Francisco* reality show. (415-551-1036; www.lovedtodeath.net; 1681-1685 Haight St; noon-7pm; 6, 7, 33, 37, 43, MN)

Piedmont Boutique

FASHION & ACCESSORIES

19 Map p132, C4

'No food, no cell phones, no playing in the boas,' says the sign at the door – but that last rule is gleefully ignored by drag stars, pageant dropouts, strippers and people who take Halloween dead seriously (read: all SF). Since 1972 Piedmont's signature getups have been designed and sewn in the city, so they're not cheap – but those airplane earrings are priceless. (415-864-8075; www.piedmontboutique.com; 1452 Haight St; 11am-7pm; 6, 7, 33, 37, 43)

Amoeba Music

Rare Device

GIFTS & SOUVENIRS

20 Map p132, F2

Sly San Francisco wit is the rare device that makes this well-curated selection of gifts for all ages so irresistible. Charcoal chef soap scrubs off leftover burrito, SF-map play mats let babies drool all over the Golden Gate Bridge, Saguaro macramé statement necklaces bring uptown fashion down to earth, and Little Otsu's un-planner finds time for joy in start-up schedules. (415-863-3969; www.raredevice.net; 600 Divisadero St; noon-8pm Mon-Fri, 11am-7pm Sat & Sun; 5, 6, 7, 21, 24)

Tantrum

TOYS

21 Map p132, B5

Overbooked kids and overworked adults deserve a time-out for Tantrum, delightfully stocked with musical otters, wooden ducks on wheels, and a mechanical seal kids can ride for a quarter. Mid-century-modern circus is the design aesthetic in new and vintage items, including stuffed circus elephants, magic bunny lamps and vintage pinafores worthy of *Alice in Wonderland*. (415-504-6980; www.shoptantrum.com; 858 Cole St; 10am-7pm; ; 6, 7, 33, 37, 43, MN)

Explore

Golden Gate Park & the Avenues

When other Americans want an extreme experience, they head to San Francisco – but when San Franciscans go to extremes, they end up here. Surfers brave walls of water on blustery Ocean Beach, runners try to keep pace with stampeding bison in Golden Gate Park, and foodies obsessively Instagram adventurous meals in the Sunset or Richmond, the family-friendly neighborhoods along the park.

The Sights in a Day

Head to **Ocean Beach** (p150) early to catch SF's daredevil surfers, then join wetsuited mavericks at **Trouble Coffee** (p152). Model local-designer hoodies at **Mollusk** (p154) before hopping the N Judah to 9th Ave to **San Francisco Botanical Garden** (p143). Hang out with blue butterflies in the rainforest dome at the **California Academy of Sciences** (p144) before sustainable dim sum lunches in the Academy Café.

Globe-trot from Egyptian goddesses to James Turrell light installations in **de Young Museum** (p146), then enjoy a Zen moment in the **Japanese Tea Garden** (p143). Summit Strawberry Hill for views over **Stow Lake** (p143) to the Pacific. Next, take bus 44 to buy gifts at **Park Life** (p154), and get the 2 Clement bus to see sculpture and radical comics at the **Legion of Honor** (p150).

Follow the trailhead from the Legion to end-of-the-world Pacific sunsets. End your evening with tropical cocktails at **Trad'r Sam** (p152), Mexican food at **Nopalito** (p152) and foot-stomping folk music at the **Plough & Stars** (p153).

Top Sights

Golden Gate Park (p142)

California Academy of Sciences (p144)

de Young Museum (p146)

Best of San Francisco

Outdoors

Golden Gate Park (p142)

Ocean Beach (p150)

Coastal Trail (p152)

San Francisco Botanical Garden (p143)

Japanese Tea Garden (p143)

Shopping

Mollusk (p154)

Park Life (p154)

Foggy Notion (p154)

Getting There

Bus Buses 1 and 38 run from downtown; 5 and 21 head along the northern edge of the park; 2 runs along Clement St; 71 follows alongside the park to the south.

M Streetcar The N train runs from downtown.

Top Sights
Golden Gate Park

Everything San Franciscans love is here: free spirits, free music, penguins, paintings, bonsai and buffalo. A stroll through the park covers 150 years of history, from Victorian Conservatory of Flowers past Hippie Hill drum circles to contemplative National AIDS Memorial Grove. Nearby, wave to penguins at California Academy of Sciences, debate art at de Young Museum and find Zen in the Japanese Tea Garden. Stop to sniff magnolias at San Francisco Botanical Garden, boat across Stow Lake and catch free Polo Fields concerts before racing bison into the sunset.

Map p148, D4

www.golden-gate-park.com

btwn Stanyan St & Great Hwy

admission free

P

5, 7, 18, 21, 28, 29, 33, 44, M N

Conservatory of Flowers

Top Sights
de Young Museum

Follow sculptor Andy Goldsworthy's artificial sidewalk fault line into Herzog & de Meuron's faultlessly sleek, copper-clad building that's oxidizing green to blend into the park. Don't be fooled by the de Young's camouflaged exterior: shows of global arts and crafts boldly broaden artistic horizons, from Oceanic ceremonial masks to James Turrell's Skyspace installation, built into a hill in the sculpture garden.

Map p148, F3

415-750-3600

http://deyoung.famsf.org

50 Hagiwara Tea Garden Dr

adult/child $15/free, 1st Tue of month free

9:30am-5:15pm Tue-Sun, to 8:45pm Fri Apr-Nov

5, 7, 44, M N

de Young Museum

Collections

The Academy's tradition of weird science dates from 1853, and today 60 research scientists and thousands of live animals coexist here. Butterflies alight on visitors in the glass rainforest dome, a rare white alligator stalks a mezzanine swamp and penguins paddle the tank in the African Hall.

Steinhart Aquarium

In the basement aquarium, kids duck inside a glass bubble to enter the Eel Forest, find Nemos in the tropical-fish tanks and befriend starfish in the aquatic petting zoo. Premier attractions include the California aquaculture wall, the walk-in tropical fish theater, columns of golden sea dragons and the huge, shy pink Pacific octopus.

Architecture

To make the Academy the world's greenest museum, Pritzker Prize–winning architect Renzo Piano creatively repurposed the original neoclassical facade while adding a 2.5-acre Living Roof, a lofty lawn polka-dotted with wildflowers, solar panels and air vents.

Morrison Planetarium

Glimpse into infinity under the massive digital projection dome, and time-travel through billions of years in a half-hour virtual journey.

Wild Nights at the Academy

After the penguins nod off to sleep, the wild rumpus starts at kids-only Academy Sleepovers. At over-21 NightLife Thursdays, rainforest-themed cocktails are served. Book ahead online.

Top Tips

- Crowds are biggest on weekends, at over-21 Thursday NightLife events (6pm to 10pm) and Academy sleepovers (6pm to 8am; ages five and up). Weekday afternoons are quieter.
- Download the Academy Insider iPhone app (free) for a self-guided tour of the Academy's collections.
- Avoid $5 surcharges applied during holidays and other peak periods by pre-ordering tickets online.

Take a Break

Academy Café offers quick bites made with sustainable ingredients, including responsibly sourced fish and humanely raised meats.

Top Sights
California Academy of Sciences

Leave it to San Francisco to dedicate a glorious four-story landmark entirely to freaks of nature. Architect Renzo Piano's LEED-certified green building in the middle of Golden Gate Park houses 40,000 weird and wondrous animals, with an indoor rainforest dome, penguin habitat and underground aquarium capped by a 'living roof' of California wildflowers.

Map p148, G3

www.calacademy.org

55 Music Concourse Dr

adult/student/child $35/30/25

9:30am-5pm Mon-Sat, from 11am Sun

P

5, 6, 7, 21, 31, 33, 44, M N

T. rex skeleton, California Academy of Sciences

Japanese Tea Garden

Since 1894, this picturesque 5-acre **garden** (☎415-752-1171; www.japaneseteagardensf.com; 75 Hagiwara Tea Garden Dr; adult/child $8/2, before 10am Mon, Wed & Fri free; ⏲9am-6pm Mar-Oct, to 4:45pm Nov-Feb; P 👪; 🚌5, 7, 44, MN) has welcomed visitors with cherry blossoms in spring, red maple leaves in fall, and green tea and fortune cookies in the Tea House.

Stow Lake

A park within the park, **Stow Lake** (www.sfrecpark.org; ⏲sunrise-sunset; 👪; 🚌7, 44, MN) offers waterfall views, picnics in the Taiwanese pagoda and bird-watching on picturesque Strawberry Hill. Pedal boats, rowboats and electric boats are available daily in good weather at the 1946 boathouse.

The Green Side of Golden Gate Park

There's always something blooming in the 70-acre **San Francisco Botanical Garden** (Strybing Arboretum; ☎415-661-1316; www.strybing.org; 1199 9th Ave; adult/child $8/2, before 9am daily & 2nd Tue of month free; ⏲7:30am-7pm Mar-Sep, to 6pm Oct–mid-Nov & Feb, to 5pm mid-Nov–Jan, last entry 1hr before closing, bookstore 10am-4pm; 👪; 🚌6, 7, 44, MN), which covers a world of vegetation from South African savanna to New Zealand cloud forest. Inside a gloriously restored 1878 Victorian greenhouse, the **Conservatory of Flowers** (☎415-831-2090 info; www.conservatoryofflowers.org; 100 John F Kennedy Dr; adult/student/child $8/6/2, 1st Tue of month free; ⏲10am-4pm Tue-Sun; 👪; 🚌5, 7, 21, 33, MN) is home to freaky outer-space orchids, contemplative floating lilies and creepy carnivorous plants.

Children's Playground

Kids have had the run of the park's southeastern end since 1887. Highlights of this historic children's playground include 1970s concrete slides, a new climbing wall and a vintage 1912 carousel.

☑ Top Tips

▶ Follow your bliss through Golden Gate Park, where great park pastimes range from disc golf and lindy-hopping to model-boat regattas and lawn bowling.

▶ Concessions inside top park attractions can add up fast for hungry families. For cheap, quick eats, look for hot-dog carts along John F Kennedy Dr or street-food trucks near the Music Concourse (between de Young Museum and California Academy of Sciences).

✕ Take a Break

On the park's western end, Beach Chalet (p153) is a pleasant parkside dining option. Just outside the park but near several top park attractions, affordable, tasty lunch options abound, including Cinderella Russian Bakery (p151).

Collection

You can see all the way from contemporary California to ancient Egypt at the globally eclectic de Young. You might spot uncanny similarities between Gerhard Richter's modern squeegee paintings and traditional Afghani rugs from the textile collection's 11,000-plus works. Upstairs, don't miss excellent modern photography and 19th-century Oceanic ceremonial oars, alongside African masks, Mesoamerican sculpture and meticulous California crafts.

Blockbuster Shows

The de Young's blockbuster basement shows range from psychedelic hand-sewn hippie fashions to Ed Ruscha paintings of Route 66 gas stations. Crowd-pleasing exhibits of fashion and treasures are consistent with the de Young's mission to showcase global arts and crafts – and art shows here are equally world-class, gorgeously presented and thoughtfully explained.

Architecture

Swiss architects Herzog & de Meuron (of Tate Modern fame) knew better than to compete with Golden Gate Park's scenery. Instead, they drew the seemingly abstract pattern of the de Young's perforated copper cladding from aerial photography of the park. The de Young's 144ft sci-fi armored tower is one architectural feature that's incongruous with the park setting – but access to the tower viewing room is free, and waiting for the elevator by Ruth Asawa's mesmerizing filigreed pods is an unexpected delight.

☑ Top Tips

- The de Young offers exceptional freebies: free admission the first Tuesday of each month, free cafe and sculpture-garden access, and free visits to the tower viewing platform.
- Fridays are an arty party with live music, performances, film premieres and artists-in-residence mingling over cocktails.
- The de Young bookstore has a smartly curated selection of one-of-a-kind jewelry, home decor and fashion.

Take a Break

Head to Nopalito (p152) at Golden Gate Park's southern border for Cal-Mex tacos, cinnamon hot chocolate and – oh yes – margaritas.

A
B
C
D
1
2
3
4
5
PACIFIC OCEAN
Land's End
Deadman's Point
China Beach
Uncle Wish Mem Rd
Coastal Trail
Point Lobos
El Camino del Mar
Legion of Honor
Lincoln Park Golf Course
Lake St
California St
32nd Ave
34th Ave
25th Ave
Lincoln Park
Fort Miley
Clement St
Point Lobos Ave
Geary Blvd
THE RICHMOND
Anza St
Sutro Heights Park
Balboa St
Upper Great Hwy
La Playa St
Fulton St
Spreckels Lake
North Lake
John F Kennedy Dr
Golden Gate Park
Golden Gate Municipal Golf Course
Golden Gate Park Equestrian Center & Stadium
Middle Dr W
Middle Lake
Metson Lake
Martin Luther King Dr
Mallard Lake
South Lake
Ocean Beach
Great Hwy
Lincoln Way
Irving St
Judah St
Sunset Blvd
Lawton St
THE SUNSET
Sunset Recreation Center

F G H

1 km
0.5 miles

Pacific Ave
Washington St
Clay St
Sacramento St
California St
Mountain Lake Park
Lake St
California St
Iris Ave
15 14 13
Clement St
6
Arguello Blvd
Palm Ave
Jordan Ave
Parker Ave
Spruce St
Cook St
4
Park Presidio Blvd
12th Ave
11th Ave
10th Ave
9th Ave
Geary Blvd
17
8th Ave
7th Ave
6th Ave
5th Ave
4th Ave
3rd Ave
2nd Ave
22nd Ave
21st Ave
20th Ave
19th Ave
18th Ave
17th Ave
16th Ave
15th Ave
Anza St
5
Rossi Playground
University of San Francisco
Balboa St
Turk Blvd
Balboa St
14th Ave
Funston Ave
University of San Francisco
Cabrillo St
Cabrillo St
Fulton St
Stanyan St
Fulton St
Conservatory Dr
de Young Museum
California Academy of Sciences
Lily Pond
Oak St
Page St
Lloyd Lake
John F Kennedy Dr
Middle Dr E
Stow Lake Dr
Stow Lake
Golden Gate Park
Elk Glen Lake
Kezar Dr
Bowling Green Dr
Lincoln Way
Frederick St
Lincoln Way
7
Hugo St
Carl St
Stanyan St
8
15th Ave
14th Ave
Funston Ave
12th Ave
6th Ave
5th Ave
Irving St
Parnassus Ave
University of California San Francisco
Judah St
7th Ave
24th Ave
23rd Ave
22nd Ave
21st Ave
20th Ave
19th Ave
18th Ave
17th Ave
16th Ave
11th Ave
10th Ave
9th Ave
8th Ave
Lawton St

2 3 4 5

For reviews see

Top Sights	p142
Sights	p150
Eating	p150
Drinking	p152
Entertainment	p153
Shopping	p154

Sights

Legion of Honor

MUSEUM

1 Map p148, B1

A museum as eccentric and illuminating as San Francisco itself, the Legion showcases a wildly eclectic collection ranging from Monet water lilies to John Cage soundscapes, ancient Iraqi ivories to R Crumb comics. Upstairs are blockbuster shows of old masters and Impressionists, but don't miss selections from the Legion's Achenbach Foundation of Graphic Arts collection of 90,000 works on paper, ranging from Rembrandt to Ed Ruscha. Ticket price includes free same-day entry to the de Young Museum (p146). (415-750-3600; http://legionofhonor.famsf.org; 100 34th Ave; adult/child $15/free, discount with Muni ticket $2, 1st Tue of month free; 9:30am-5:15pm Tue-Sun; ; 1, 2, 18, 38)

Ocean Beach

BEACH

2 Map p148, A4

Most days are too chilly for bikini-clad clambakes but fine for hardy beachcombers and hardcore surfers braving riptides (casual swimmers, beware). The original site of Burning Man, Ocean Beach now allows bonfires only in 16 artist-designed fire pits until 9:30pm; no alcohol permitted. Stick to paths in the fragile southern dunes, where skittish snowy plover shorebirds shelter in winter. (415-561-4323; www.parksconservancy.org; Great Hwy; sunrise-sunset; P; 5, 18, 31, MN)

Eating

Outerlands

CALIFORNIAN $$

3 Map p148, B5

When windy Ocean Beach leaves you feeling shipwrecked, drift into this beach-shack bistro for organic Californian comfort food. Brunch demands Dutch pancakes in iron skillets with housemade ricotta, lunch brings cast-iron-grilled artisan cheese on house-baked levain bread with citrusy Steely Dan–themed beach cocktails, and dinner means creative coastal fare like hazelnut-dusted California salmon with black-eyed peas. Reserve. (415-661-6140; www.outerlandssf.com; 4001 Judah St; sandwiches & small plates $8-14, mains $15-27; 9am-3pm & 5-10pm; ; 18, MN)

Dragon Beaux

DIM SUM $$

4 Map p148, E2

Hong Kong meets Vegas at SF's most glamorous, decadent Cantonese restaurant. Say yes to cartloads of succulent roast meats – hello, roast duck and pork belly – and creative dumplings, especially XO dumplings with plump, brandy-laced shrimp in spinach wrappers. Expect premium teas, sharp service and impeccable Cantonese standards, like Chinese doughnuts, *har gow* (shrimp dumplings) and Chinese broccoli in oyster sauce. (415-333-8899; www.dragonbeaux.com; 5700 Geary Blvd; dumplings $4-9; 11:30am-2:30pm & 5:30-10pm Mon-Thu, to 10:30pm Fri, 10am-3pm & 5:30-10pm Sat & Sun; ; 2, 38)

SHUTTERSTOCK ©

Legion of Honor

Cinderella Russian Bakery

RUSSIAN $

5 Map p148, G2

Fog banks and cold wars are no match for the heartwarming powers of the Cinderella, serving treats like your baba used to make since 1953. Join SF's Russian community in Cinderella's new parklet near Golden Gate Park for scrumptious, just-baked egg-and-green-onion piroshki, hearty borscht and decadent dumplings – all at neighborly prices. (415-751-6723; www.cinderellabakery.com; 436 Balboa St; pastries $1.50-3.50, mains $7-13; 7am-7pm; ; 5, 21, 31, 33)

Wako

SUSHI, JAPANESE $$$

6 Map p148, G2

Tiny yet mighty in fascination, chef-owner Tomoharu Nakamura's driftwood-paneled bistro is as quirkily San Franciscan as the bonsai grove at the nearby Japanese Tea Garden (p143). Each *omakase* (chef's choice) dish is a miniature marvel of Japanese seafood with a California accent – Santa Cruz abalone *nigiri*, seared tuna belly with California caviar, crab *mushimono* with yuzu grown by a neighbor. *Domo arigato*, dude. (415-682-4875; www.sushiwakosf.com; 211 Clement St; 9-course menu $95; 5:30-10pm Mon-Thu; 1, 2, 33, 38, 44)

Local Life

Coasting the Coast

Hit your stride on the **Coastal Trail** (Map p148, B1; www.californiacoastaltrail.info; sunrise-sunset; 1, 18, 38) along sandy Ocean Beach, then follow the Presidio coastline to the Golden Gate Bridge. Casual strollers can pick up the trail near Sutro Baths, head around Land's End for end-of-the-world views, then duck into the Legion of Honor at Lincoln Park.

Nopalito

MEXICAN $$

7 Map p148, G4

Head south of Golden Gate Park's border for upscale, sustainably sourced Cal-Mex, including succulent Sonoma-duck empanadas, melt-in-your-mouth *carnitas* (beer-braised pork) with handmade organic-corn tortillas, and cinnamon-laced Mexican hot chocolate. Reservations are not accepted, but at sunny weekends when every parkgoer craves margaritas and ceviche, call to join the waiting list an hour ahead or pre-order online. (415-233-9966; www.nopalitosf.com; 1224 9th Ave; mains $13-21; 11:30am-10pm; 6, 7, 43, 44, MN)

Revenge Pies

DESSERTS $

8 Map p148, G4

Living well is only the second-best revenge – a face full of pecan Revenge Pie is far more satisfying. Here's the compensation for every skimpy à la mode serving you've suffered through: picecream (homemade frozen custard with flakes of buttery pie crust). The chocolate-almond Revenge pie is a crowd-pleaser – but the key-lime picecream could make, break and remake friendships. Inside San Franpsycho (p155). (www.revengepies.com; 1248 9th Ave; pie $5-8, picecream $3-6; 9am-9pm; 6, 7, 43, 44, MN)

Drinking

Trad'r Sam

BAR

9 Map p148, D2

Island getaways at this vintage tiki dive will make you forget that Ocean Beach chill. Sailor-strength hot buttered rum will leave you three sheets to the wind, and five-rum Zombies will leave you wondering what happened to your brain. Kitsch-lovers order the Hurricane, which comes with two straws for a reason: drink it solo and it'll blow you away. (415-221-0773; 6150 Geary Blvd; 9am-2am; 1, 29, 31, 38)

Trouble Coffee & Coconut Club

CAFE

10 Map p148, B5

Coconuts are unlikely near blustery Ocean Beach, but here comes Trouble with the 'Build Your Own Damn House' breakfast special: coffee, thick-cut cinnamon-laced toast and an entire young coconut. Join surfers sipping house roasts on driftwood perches outside, or toss back espresso in stoneware cups at the reclaimed-wood counter. Featured on National

Public Radio, but not Instagram – sorry, no indoor photos. (4033 Judah St; 7am-7pm; 18, N)

Beach Chalet

BREWERY, BAR

11 Map p148, A4

Microbrews with views: watch Pacific sunsets through pint glasses of the Beach Chalet's Riptide Red ale, with live music most Fridays and Saturdays. Downstairs, splendid 1930s Works Project Administration (WPA) frescoes celebrate the building of Golden Gate Park. The backyard Park Chalet hosts raucous Taco Tuesdays, lazy Sunday brunch buffets, and $1 oysters during happy hour (3pm to 6pm Wednesday to Friday). (415-386-8439; www.beachchalet.com; 1000 Great Hwy; 9am-10pm Mon-Thu, to midnight Fri, 8am-midnight Sat, to 11pm Sun; ; 5, 18, 31)

Tommy's Mexican Restaurant

BAR

12 Map p148, D2

Welcome to SF's temple of tequila since 1965. Tommy's serves enchiladas as a cover for day drinking until 7pm, when margarita pitchers with *blanco, reposado or añejo* tequila rule. Cuervo Gold is displayed 'for educational purposes only' – it doesn't meet Tommy's strict criteria of unadulterated 100% agave, preferably aged in small barrels. Luckily for connoisseurs, 311 tasty tequilas do. (415-387-4747; http://tommysmexican.com; 5929 Geary Blvd; noon-11pm Wed-Mon; 1, 29, 31, 38)

Entertainment

Plough & Stars

LIVE MUSIC

13  Map p148, G2

Bands who sell out shows from Ireland to Appalachia and headline SF's **Hardly Strictly Bluegrass festival** (www.hardlystrictlybluegrass.com; Oct) jam here on weeknights, taking breaks to clink pint glasses of Guinness at long union-hall tables. Mondays compensate for no live music with an all-day happy hour, plus free pool

Top Tip

Freewheeling Through the Park

To cover the entire 48-block stretch of the Golden Gate Park, rent bikes at park-adjacent **San Francyclo** (Map p148, H3; 415-831-8031; http://sanfrancyclo.com; 746 Arguello Blvd; rental bike per hour incl helmet $10-40; 11am-7pm Mon-Fri, 10am-5pm Sat & Sun; ; 5, 21, 31, 33, 38) or skates at **Golden Gate Park Bike & Skate** (Map p148, G3; 415-668-1117; www.goldengateparkbikeandskate.com; 3038 Fulton St; skates per hr $5-6, per day $20-24, bikes per hr $3-5, per day $15-25, tandem bikes per hr/day $15/75, discs $6/25; 10am-6pm Mon-Fri, to 7pm Sat & Sun; ; 5, 21, 31, 44). Sundays year-round, Golden Gate Park's John F Kennedy Dr closes to traffic east of Crossover Dr to accommodate cyclists and skaters.

Understand
The Fog Belt

Not sure what to wear to a day in Golden Gate Park or dinner in the Avenues? Welcome to San Francisco's fog belt, where coastal fog drops temperatures by up to 20°F (10°C) on the short trip from downtown – you might need a wool coat here in July. To assess the fog situation, view satellite imagery on the National Oceanic & Atmospheric Administration (NOAA) website (www.wrh.noaa.gov/mtr). When the fog wears out its welcome, head to sunnier spots in the Castro or Mission – or hop BART to sunny Berkeley across the bay.

and blarney from regulars; expect modest cover charges ($6 to $14) for barnstorming weekend shows. (☎415-751-1122; www.theploughandstars.com; 116 Clement St; ⏰3pm-2am Mon-Thu, from 2pm Fri-Sun, shows 9pm; 🚌1, 2, 33, 38, 44)

Shopping

Park Life GIFTS & SOUVENIRS

14 Map p148, G2

The Swiss Army knife of hip SF emporiums, Park Life is design store, indie publisher and art gallery all in one. Browse presents too clever to give away, including toy soldiers in yoga poses, Tauba Auerbach's reprogrammed Casio watches, Park Life catalogs of Shaun O'Dell paintings of natural disorder and sinister Todd Hido photos of shaggy cats on shag rugs. (☎415-386-7275; www.parklifestore.com; 220 Clement St; ⏰11am-8pm Mon-Sat, to 6pm Sun; 🚌1, 2, 33, 38, 44)

Foggy Notion GIFTS & SOUVENIRS

15 Map p148, G2

You can't take Golden Gate Park home with you – the city would seem naked without it – but Foggy Notion specializes in sense memories of SF's urban wilderness. The all-natural, all-artisan gift selection includes Juniper Ridge's hiking-trail scents, Golden Gate Park honey, SF artist Julia Canright's hand-printed canvas backpacks, and Wildman beard conditioner for scruff soft as fog. (☎415-683-5654; www.foggy-notion.com; 275 6th Ave; ⏰11am-7pm Mon-Sat, to 6pm Sun; 🚌1, 2, 38, 49)

Mollusk SPORTS & OUTDOORS

16 Map p148, B4

The geodesic-dome tugboat marks the spot where ocean meets art in this surf gallery. Legendary shapers (surfboard makers) create limited-edition boards for Mollusk, and signature big-wave T-shirts and hoodies win nods of recognition on Ocean Beach. Kooks (newbies) get vicarious thrills from coffee-table books on California surf culture, Thomas Campbell ocean collages and other works by SF surfer-artists. (☎415-564-6300; www.mollusksurfshop.com; 4500 Irving St; ⏰10am-6:30pm Mon-Sat, to 6pm Sun; 🚌18, Ⓜ N)

Ocean Beach (p150)

Jade Chocolates

FOOD

17 Map p148, G2

SF-born chocolatier Mindy Fong hits the sweet spot between East and West with only-in-SF treats like passion-fruit caramels, Thai-curry hot chocolate and the legendary peanut Buddha with mango jam. Fusion flavors originally inspired by Fong's pregnancy cravings have won national acclaim, but Jade keeps its SF edge with experimental chocolates featuring sriracha, California's homegrown, Asian-inspired chili sauce. (415-350-3878; www.jadechocolates.com; 4207 Geary Blvd; 11am-7pm Tue-Sat; 2, 31, 38, 44)

San Franpsycho

GIFTS & SOUVENIRS

Blow minds with souvenirs that get visitors mistaken for locals (see 8 Map p148, G4). Be the toast of Golden Gate Park concerts with California origami-bear flasks, and go from downtown protests to beach bonfires in tees featuring the Golden Gate Bridge and the city's unofficial slogan: 'Build bridges, not walls.' Complete Cali-casual looks with driftwood jewelry and matching hoodies for you and your dog. (415-213-5442; http://sanfranpsycho.com; 1248 9th Ave; 10am-9pm; ; 6, 7, 43, 44, MN)

The Best of **San Francisco**

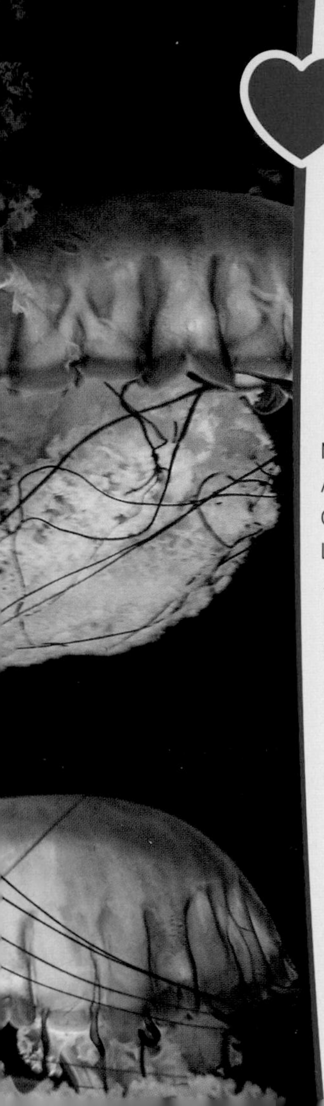

San Francisco's Best Walks

San Francisco's Best...

Jellyfish in a San Francisco aquarium
ETHAN DANIELS/SHUTTERSTOCK ©

Best Walks
Haight Flashback

The Walk

Whether you're a hippie born too late, a punk born too early, or a weirdo who passes as normal, Haight St is here to claim you as its own. On this walk you'll cover 100 years of Haight history, starting in 1867 with the park that was San Francisco's saving grace in the disastrous 1906 earthquake and fire. Fog and grit come with the scenery, but there's no better place to break away from the everyday and find your nonconformist niche.

Start Buena Vista Park; Haight St

Finish Golden Gate Park; Stanyan St

Length 1.3 miles; one hour

Take a Break

What a long, strange trip it's been – refuel with a burger and beer at **Magnolia Brewery** (p136), the microbrewery and organic eatery named after a Grateful Dead song.

SHOOTANYWHERE/SHUTTERSTOCK ©

Corner of Haight & Ashbury (p134)

❶ Buena Vista Park

Start your trip back in time in **Buena Vista Park** (p134), where San Franciscans found refuge from the earthquake and fire of 1906, and watched their town burn for three days.

❷ Bound Together Anarchist Book Collective

Heading west, you may recognize Emma Goldman and Sacco and Vanzetti in the mural at **1369 Haight St**. If not, bookstore staff can provide you with some biographical comics to introduce you.

❸ SLA Safehouse

At **1235 Masonic Ave**, you might once have glimpsed the Symbionese Liberation Army. Local legend claims this was once a safehouse where they held Patty Hearst, the kidnapped heiress turned revolutionary bank robber.

❹ Grateful Dead House

Pay your respects to the former flophouse of Jerry Garcia, Bob Weir,

Pigpen and sundry Deadheads at **710 Ashbury St**.

❺ Janis Joplin's Crash Pad

Down the block, **635 Ashbury St** is one of many Haight addresses for Janis Joplin, who had a hard time hanging onto leases in the 1960s – but as she sang, 'freedom's just another word for nothin' left to lose.'

❻ Haight & Ashbury

At the corner of **Haight & Ashbury** (p134) the clock overhead always reads 4:20, better known in 'Hashbury' as International Bong-Hit Time.

❼ Jimi's Jams

The Victorian at **1524 Haight St** was a notorious hippie flophouse, where Jimi Hendrix crashed in his 'Purple Haze' days. Fittingly, it is now a head shop; the next-door music store sells a lot of guitars.

❽ Hippie Hill

Follow the beat of your own drum to the **Hippie Hill** drum circle in Golden Gate Park – 40 years since it started, free spirits haven't entirely agreed on a rhythm. Notice the shaggy 'Janis Joplin Tree' – squint hard, and it resembles the singer's wild-haired profile.

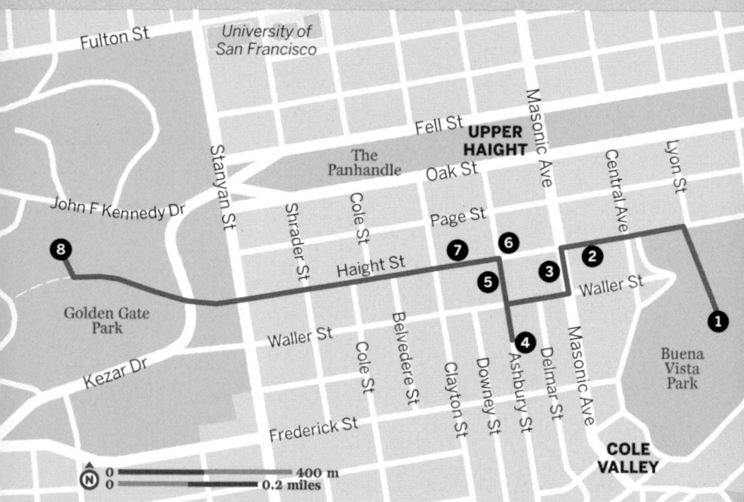

Best Walks
North Beach Beat

The Walk

Poetry is in the air and on the sidewalk on this literary tour of North Beach featuring legendary City Lights bookstore, home of Beat poetry and free speech. It's an easy walk, but you'll want at least a couple of hours to see the neighborhood as *On the Road* author Jack Kerouac did – with drinks at the beginning, middle and end.

Start Bob Kaufman Alley; Columbus Ave

Finish Li Po; Kearny St

Length 1.5 miles; two hours

Take a Break

Hot out of the century-old oven, the focaccia at **Liguria Bakery** (p62) is equal parts flour, water and poetry.

KRIS DAVIDSON/LONELY PLANET ©

Vesuvio (p65)

1 Bob Kaufman Alley

This quiet alley is named for the legendary street-corner poet who cofounded *Beatitudes* magazine in 1959, but took a vow of silence after Kennedy's assassination. He didn't speak again until the Vietnam War ended, when he walked into a North Beach cafe and recited 'All Those Ships that Never Sailed'.

2 Caffe Trieste

Order a potent espresso, check out the opera on the jukebox and slide into the back booth under the Sardinian fishing mural, where Francis Ford Coppola drafted the screenplay for *The Godfather*. **Caffe Trieste** (p65) has been a neighborhood institution since 1956, with the local characters and bathroom-wall poetry to prove it.

3 City Lights

'Abandon all despair, all ye who enter,' reads a sign by poet-founder Lawrence Ferlinghetti at **City Lights** (p58). This commandment is easy to follow upstairs in the

sunny Poetry Room, with its piles of freshly published verse. Rest in the Poet's Chair, and read a poem to inspire your journey through literary North Beach.

❹ Beat Museum

Don't be surprised to hear a Dylan jam session by the front door, or glimpse Allen Ginsberg naked in documentary footage screened inside the **Beat Museum** (p59); the Beat goes on here in rare form.

❺ Specs Museum Cafe

Begin your literary bar crawl at **Specs** (p64) amid merchant-marine memorabilia, tall tales and a glass of Anchor Steam.

❻ Jack Kerouac Alley

On the Road author Jack Kerouac once blew off Henry Miller to go on a bender, until **Vesuvio** (p65) bartenders ejected him into the street now named for him: **Jack Kerouac Alley** (p60). Note the words of Chinese poet Li Po embedded in the alley: 'In the company of friends, there is never enough wine.'

❼ Li Po Cocktails

Follow the literary lead of Kerouac and Ginsberg and end your night under the laughing Buddha at **Li Po** (p65). There may not be enough wine among friends, but there's plenty of beer.

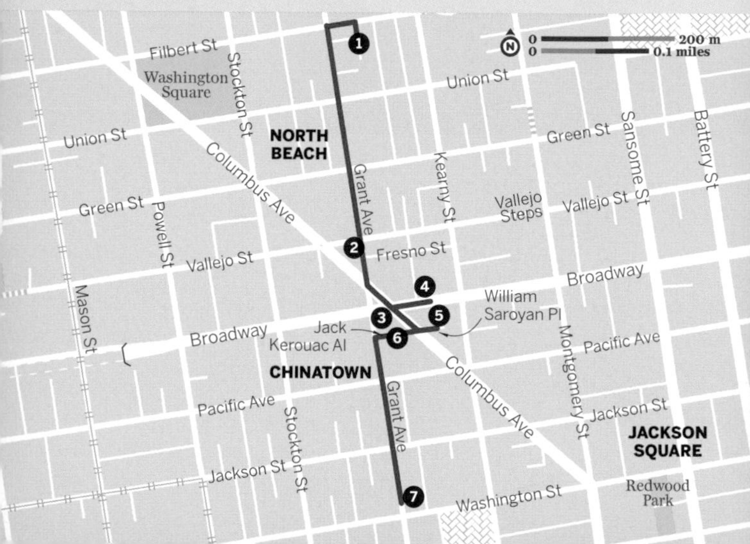

Best
Eating Out

Other US cities boast bigger monuments, but San Francisco packs more flavor. With more restaurants per capita than any other North American city (sorry, New York), San Francisco spoils diners for choice. Almost anything grows in California's fertile farmland, so SF's top chefs have an unfair advantage with local, organic, flavor-bursting ingredients.

Fusion Flair

Benu Fine dining meets DJ styling: ingenious remixes of Eastern classics with the best ingredients in the West. (p86)

Namu Gaji Organic, Korean-inspired, Sonoma-grown soul food at communal tables. (p118)

Ichi Sushi Sustainable seafood dressed to impress with California ingredients. (p119)

Top Chefs for Less

Cotogna Rustic Italian from 2011 James Beard Award–winner Michael Tusk. (p61)

Mijita *Iron Chef* winner and *Top Chef Masters* finalist Traci Des Jardins honors her grandmother's casual Mexican cooking. (p75)

Tout Sweet *Top Chef Just Desserts* winner Yigit Pura gives French macarons California humor and wit – get the PB&J. (p86)

California's Wild Side

Coi Wild tasting menus featuring foraged morels, wildflowers and Pacific seafood. (p61)

Rich Table Freestyling California fare with French finesse. (p102)

Al's Place California dreaming starts with imaginative plates of pristine Pacific seafood and heirloom NorCal specialties. (p118)

ANDREW MONTGOMERY/LONELY PLANET ©

☑ Top Tips

- On weekends reservations are usually mandatory, unless you want to eat before 6pm or after 9:30pm.
- Most SF restaurants offer reservations online through OpenTable (www.opentable.com). If the system shows no availability, try calling the restaurant directly.
- SF's top tables are mostly California casual: jeans are acceptable, welcomes warm rather than formal, and servers informative to the point of chatty.

Ferry Plaza Farmers Market (p75)

Date-Night Favorites

Boulevard Chef Nancy Oakes' hearty, unfussy Californian fare may be the reason you leave your heart in SF. (p87)

Jardinière Behind the opera, chef Traci Des Jardins hits all the right notes – decadent, smart, sustainable – with a slight Italian accent. (p102)

Gary Danko Escape from Alcatraz for romance served in leisurely, luxuriant courses. (p43)

Casual Dates

Outerlands Organic surfer lunches hearty enough to take on big waves. (p150)

Dragon Beaux If you're willing to share these brandy-laced XO dumplings, it must be love. (p150)

Food Trucks & Market Stalls

Off the Grid Up to 30 food trucks provide a movable feast, from curry to cupcakes. (p30)

Ferry Plaza Farmers Market Graze on organic peaches, Sonoma goat's cheese and Korean tacos. (p75)

Heart of the City Farmers Market DIY lunches of roast chicken, organic berries, gourmet doughnuts and more. (p103)

Hot Deals

La Taqueria Where SF's most memorable meals come wrapped in foil and under $9 – including spicy pickles. (p118)

Liguria Bakery Foccacia fresh from the century-old oven. (p62)

Z & Y Sichuan specialties poached in flaming chili oil numb lips and blow minds. (p62)

Udupi Palace South Indian in the Mission – SF's definitive *dosa* (lentil pancake). (p120)

Cinderella Russian Bakery Hot piroshki (pocket pastries) in a cool parklet. (p151)

Rosamunde Sausage Grill Sausages with free gourmet fixings and next-door microbrews. (p135)

Best Drinks

Ban 'the usual' from your drinking vocabulary – you won't find that here. The Gold Rush brought a rush on the bar; by 1850 San Francisco had 500 saloons supplied by local brewers, distillers and Sonoma vineyards. Today California's homegrown traditions of wine, beer and cocktails are converging in saloon revivals, award-winning wines and microbrewery booms.

History in the Making

In the Barbary Coast days, cocktails were used to sedate sailors and shanghai them onto outbound ships. Now bartenders are researching local recipes and reviving old SF traditions, pouring rye and homemade bitters over hand-hewn ice cubes, whipping egg whites into Pisco sours, and apparently still trying to knock sailors cold with combinations of tawny port and agricole rum served in punch bowls.

If you order a martini, you may get the original, invented-in-SF version: vermouth, gin, bitters, lemon, maraschino cherry and ice. All that authenticity-tripping may sound self-conscious, but after strong pours at California's vintage saloons, consciousness is hardly an issue.

Museums After Hours

Museums offer some of SF's wildest nights out. NightLife at California Academy of Sciences has rainforest-themed cocktails every Thursday night. Exploratorium offers mad-scientist glow-in-the-dark cocktails at After Dark events, while the de Young Museum invites you to mingle with artists-in-residence over art-themed cocktails at first Friday openings.

ANDREW MONTGOMERY/LONELY PLANET ©

Speakeasies

Local Edition This just in: sensational cocktails cause stir in basement of the Hearst newspaper building. (p88)

Smuggler's Cove Roll with the rum punches at this Barbary Coast shipwreck bar hidden behind tinted glass. (p105)

Bourbon & Branch Not since Prohibition have secret passwords and gin knowledge been this handy. (p106)

Dalva & Hideout Hidden back-bar cocktails feature housemade bitters and intriguing names – get the Dirty Pigeon. (p121)

California Wine

20 Spot Instant mellow, with Eames rockers,

deviled duck eggs and 100 wines. (p120)

West Coast Wine & Cheese Pairing local cheese with 26 California, Oregon and Washington wines by the glass. (p31)

Saloons

Comstock Saloon Vintage Barbary Coast saloon with potent concoctions and dainty bar bites. (p64)

Elixir Organic, local drinks in a Wild West, green-certified saloon. (p121)

Rickhouse Impeccable bourbon drinks in a chic shotgun-shack setting downtown. (p88)

Drink Think Tanks

Bar Agricole Valedictorian cocktails, with James Beard accolades and double major in history and rum. (p88)

Trick Dog Every six months the cocktail menu reflects a new SF obsession – landmark buildings, say, or Chinese diners. (p120)

Rye Alcohol alchemy: exact ratios of obscure bitters, small-batch liquor and fresh-squeezed juices. (p105)

Alembic Old Tom gin genius and gourmet bites for aficionados. (p137)

Epic Dives

Specs Drink like a sailor at this hideaway plastered with Seven Seas mementos. (p64)

Hemlock Tavern Peanuts and punk rock, plus near-impossible trivia nights. (p108)

Edinburgh Castle Literary pub with readings, darts and a thick Scottish accent. (p105)

Lounges

Tosca Cafe Warm up from the inside out with jukebox opera and spiked espresso drinks. (p62)

Aub Zam Zam Persian jazz lounge with bargain cocktails in the Haight. (p136)

Beer

Zeitgeist Beer garden with surly female bartenders tapping 40 microbrews. (p122)

Toronado Beer for every season and any reason – summer ales, holiday barley wines, Oktoberfest wheats. (p136)

Irish Bank Downtown's secret Emerald Isle getaway offers properly poured Guinness and fish and chips in cozy snugs. (p89)

ANDREW MONTGOMERY/LONELY PLANET ©

Beach Chalet Microbrews with views of Ocean Beach, WPA murals downstairs, and bands in the backyard. (p153)

Cafes

Caffe Trieste The soul of North Beach: poets, directors, accordion jams and espresso. (p65)

Ritual Coffee Roasters Heady roasts, local art and seats among burlap coffee bags in a cult roastery-cafe. (p122)

Best LGBT

Doesn't matter where you're from, who you love or who's your daddy: if you're here and queer, welcome home. Singling out the best places to be out in San Francisco is almost redundant. Though the Castro is a gay hub and the Mission is a magnet for lesbians, the entire city is gay friendly – hence the number of out elected representatives in City Hall.

LGBT Nightlife

New York Marys may label SF the retirement home of the young – the sidewalks do roll up early – but honey, SF's drag glitter nuns need their beauty rest between throwing Hunky Jesus contests and running for public office. Most thump-thump clubs are concentrated not in the lesbian-magnet Mission or historic gay Castro, but in SoMa warehouses, where dancing queens, playgrrrls and leather scenesters can make some noise. In the 1950s bars euphemistically designated Sunday afternoons as 'tea dances,' appealing to gay crowds to make money at an otherwise slow time – and Sundays remain SF's busiest.

SF Pride Month

No one shows Pride like San Francisco. The world's most extravagant celebration lasts all of June, kicking off with 200 film screenings at the San Francisco LGBTQ Film Festival (www.frameline.org), gearing up with Dyke March & Pink Party (www.dykemarch.org) and ending in the joyous, 1.2-million-strong Lesbian, Gay, Bisexual & Transgender Pride Parade (www.sfpride.org).

JOHN S LANDER/GETTY IMAGES ©

Top Tip

- Enjoy public spankings for local charities on the last Sunday in September at the **Folsom Street Fair** (www.folsomstreetfair.com; Sep), a clothing-optional leather fair.
- Check out the **Sisters of Perpetual Indulgence** (www.thesisters.org) calendar for costumed fundraising extravaganzas, including the Hunky Jesus contest on Easter Sunday.

Classic Bars

Eagle Tavern Landmark SoMa leather rocker bar, as friendly/sleazy as you wanna be. (p89)

San Francisco LGBT Pride Parade

Twin Peaks Tavern The first gay bar with windows; now there's a neon rainbow. Toast to progress. (p129)

Women into Women

Cat Club Retro '90s twisted Bondage-a-Go-Go and totally rad '80s Thursdays. (p88)

Rickshaw Stop Something for everyone, SF-style: lesbian disco, Bollywood mash-ups, Latin spice. (p106)

El Rio Oyster happy hours, air hockey, slick DJ mixes and SF's flirtiest patio. (p120)

Dance Clubs

EndUp Ride the beat from Ghetto Disco Saturdays to Monday-morning sunrises over the freeway. (p89)

DNA Lounge Known for booty-shaking mash-ups, burlesque, Goth and live acts: Prince played here. (p91)

Drag

Oasis Drag acts so outrageous, you'll laugh until you cough up glitter. (p90)

Aunt Charlie's Lounge Knock-down, drag-out winner for gender-bending shows and dance-floor freakiness. (p105)

By Day

GLBT History Museum The first gay-history museum in America, in the heart of history-making Castro. (p129)

Dolores Park Sun and cityscapes on a grassy southwest slope nicknamed Gay Beach, plus a playground for families. (p113)

Women's Building Glorious murals crown this community institution. (p113)

Party Supplies

Mr S Leather Spiked dog collars, PVC hoods and, oh yes, leather. (p93)

Piedmont Boutique Faux-fur hot pants, glitter leg warmers and a boa... done! (p138)

Best Museums & Galleries

Museums

de Young Museum Golden Gate Park's global arts-and-crafts showcase. (p146)

Asian Art Museum Trip through 6000 years and 4000 miles in an hour, with masterpieces from Mumbai to Tokyo. (p96)

California Academy of Sciences Chase butterflies under the rainforest dome or shuffle with the penguins inside this living museum. (p144)

Exploratorium Trippy hands-on exhibits test scientific theories and blow minds at Pier 15. (p51)

Contemporary Jewish Museum Artworks by Warhol, Houdini, Lou Reed and Gertrude Stein prove great minds don't always think alike. (p84)

San Francisco Museum of Modern Art Expand horizons with expanded contemporary collections in SF's supersized art museum. (p80)

History

Alcatraz Tour the notorious island prison, from solitary cells to attempted escape routes. (p49)

USS Pampanito Dive into history inside this WWII submarine. (p37)

California Historical Society Gold Rush telegrams, earthquake photos, psychedelic rock posters and other SF ephemera. (p84)

Murals

Coit Tower Murals showing SF during the Great Depression got 26 artists labeled first communists, then national treasures. (p54)

Balmy Alley The Mission muralist movement started here. (p116)

Diego Rivera Gallery The mural maestro pauses to admire SF in progress in this fresco self-portrait. (p42)

Maritime Museum WPA murals of surreal sea life line this monumental

MARIUSZ S. JURGIELEWICZ/SHUTTERSTOCK ©

hint to sailors in need of a scrub. (p41)

Contemporary Art Galleries

49 Geary Four floors of galleries covering all media, from interactive environmental art to classic silver-gelatin photographs. (p85)

Luggage Store Gallery Street art comes in from the cold at this breakthrough art nonprofit. (p100)

Adobe Books & Backroom Gallery Art made on-site by the artist in residence, plus art books and zines galore. (p126)

Best Architecture

Superman wouldn't be so impressive in San Francisco, where most buildings are small enough for a middling superhero to leap in a single bound. But San Francisco's low-profile buildings are its highlights, from original adobe and gabled Victorians to flower-topped museums.

Iconic Landmarks

Golden Gate Bridge Orange deco span with the best disappearing act on the planet. (p24)

Coit Tower The white exclamation point on SF's skyline is dedicated to firefighters and lined with exclamation-worthy murals. (p54)

Palace of Fine Arts Idealists leap to rescue art atop Bernard Maybeck's romantic neoclassical monument. (p28)

Ferry Building The clock tower atop this 1898 building welcomes visitors from both the water and dry land. (p74)

Victorians

Alamo Square Park Picture-perfect snapshot of SF Victorian architecture, from Queen Annes to Sticks. (p134)

Grateful Dead House Little could the Victorians predict what this home would become in the '60s. (p134)

Modern Marvels

California Academy of Sciences The world's first Platinum LEED-certified green museum, designed by Renzo Piano – capped with a living wildflower roof. (p144)

de Young Museum Herzog & de Meuron's copper-clad building is oxidizing green, blending into park scenery. (p146)

San Francisco Museum of Modern Art Mario Botta's brick-boxed lightwell has a radical new extension by Snøhetta architects. (p80)

LYNN Y/SHUTTERSTOCK ©

☑ Top Tip

▶ Stick-style architecture (1870–80s) is characterized by flat fronts and long, narrow windows; see the Mission.

▶ Queen Anne style (1880s–1910) resulted in exuberant turreted, gabled mansions; see the Haight.

▶ Edwardian architecture (1901–14) typically includes false gables and arts-and-crafts details; see the Avenues.

Best Outdoors

If the climb doesn't take your breath away, the scenery surely will. Nature has been kind to San Francisco, but it's taken generations of conservation efforts to preserve this splendor. Early champions include Sierra Club founder John Muir, Golden Gate Park planner William Hammond Hall, and ordinary San Franciscans who saw beauty and not just gold in these hills.

San Francisco's Green Outlook

According to the North American Green Cities Index, San Francisco is the greenest of them all. Practices that are standard-setting elsewhere were pioneered here, including LEED-certified green hotels, organic cocktail bars, sustainable dining from tacos to tasting menus, and dozens of car-parking spaces that have been converted into public green oases. San Francisco mandates citywide composting and bans plastic bags – part of its initiative to become a zero-waste city by 2020.

Wheels & Waves

Daredevil hills and dazzling waves invite SF visitors to roll, surf and sail around town. Haight St is street-skateboarding at its obstacle-course best, and disco-skaters roll in Golden Gate Park on Sundays.

Bone-chilling Pacific riptides are not for novices; check the **surf report** (☎415-273-1618) before you suit up. Sailing is best April through August, but whale-watching season peaks mid-October through December.

MIZZICK/SHUTTERSTOCK ©

Hilltop Vistas

Coit Tower Parrot's-eye views over the bay along garden-lined stairways, and from the tower's viewing platform. (p54)

Alamo Square Park Downtown vistas trimmed with lacy Victorian rooflines. (p134)

Beaches & Waterfront

Crissy Field The retired military airstrip is now patrolled by windsurfers, shorebirds, joggers and puppies. (p28)

Golden Gate Park (p142)

Ocean Beach Beachcombers, surfers and serious sandcastle architects brave SF's blustery Pacific Ocean Beach. (p150)

Baker Beach Golden Gate Bridge views and clothing-optional sunbathing on a former army base. (p28)

Outdoor Activities

Golden Gate Park All of San Francisco's favorite pastimes in one place: baseball, biking, rocking out and lollygagging. (p142)

Coastal Trail Cover 9 miles of waterfront from Fort Funston to Fort Mason, with sparkling Pacific and bay views. (p152)

Urban Wildlife

Sea lions at Pier 39 This harem features more posturing, clowning and infighting than a reality TV show. (p37)

Wild parrots at Coit Tower The renegade parrots that turn treetops red, yellow, green and blue around SF's white tower. (p54)

Bison in Golden Gate Park See the smallest stampede in the West run full tilt toward park windmills. (p142)

Botanical Wonders

San Francisco Botanical Garden Explore the world inside Golden Gate Park, from California redwoods to South African savannas. (p143)

Japanese Tea Garden Contemplate priceless lost-and-found bonsai over iron pots of tea. (p143)

Best Live Music

Classical & Opera

San Francisco Symphony Edge-of-your-seat, Grammy-winning performances. (p107)

San Francisco Opera Divas bring down the house with reinvented classics and original works like Stephen King's *Dolores Claiborne*. (p107)

Jazz, Bluegrass & Folk

SFJAZZ Center Top talents reinvent standards and find fresh inspiration in mariachis, skateboarding and Hunter S Thompson. (p106)

Plough & Stars Major bluegrass and folk bands pack Irish pub benches. (p153)

Hotel Utah Saloon Twangy indie bands and singer-songwriters get toes tapping in this genuine-article Wild West saloon. (p91)

Rock, R&B & Pop

Great American Music Hall A former bordello now hosts red-hot acts, from alt-rock legends and baroque poppers to world music. (p107)

Warfield Marquee acts get balconies roaring at this former vaudeville theater. (p108)

Bimbo's 365 Club Top 40 names and retro rockers play a historic speakeasy. (p67)

Independent This compact venue features indie dreamers, offbeat comedians and alt-pop stars. (p137)

Mezzanine Street cred and sound quality – West Coast rap and throwback bands on the comeback trail. (p91)

Beach Chalet Music with a sunset backdrop on Fridays and Saturdays. (p153)

STEVE JENNINGS/GETTY IMAGES ©

Top Tips

▸ Bargain tickets are sold on the day of the performance for cash only at TIX Bay Area (www.tixbayarea.org). Otherwise, try SF-based Craig's List (www.craigslist.org).

Best Shopping

All those tricked-out dens, well-stocked spice racks and fabulous ensembles don't just pull themselves together – San Franciscans scour their city for them. Eclectic originality is San Francisco's signature style, and that's not one-stop shopping. But consider the thrill of the hunt: while shopping in SF, you can watch fish theater, make necklaces from zippers and trade fashion tips with drag queens.

Cali Lifestyle

826 Valencia Pirate supplies to defend SF against scurvy, boredom and Oakland Raiders. (p116)

Piedmont Boutique Cross-dress to impress with locally designed drag fabulousness. (p138)

Park Life Instant street smarts, from local-artist designed tees to original works by SF graffiti artists. (p154)

Little Paper Planes Original gifts by indie makers, gallery-ready clothing and works on paper from LPP's artist's residency program. (p125)

Local Maker

Heath Ceramics Pottery purveyor to star chefs since 1948. (p126)

Mollusk Surf legends shop here for artist-designed hoodies, T-shirts and hand-shaped surfboards. (p154)

Foggy Notion California chalkboards, Golden Gate Park honey and other SF-made novelties. (p154)

Nancy Boy Overachieving beauty products, locally made with effective natural ingredients. (p108)

Gourmet Gifts

Recchiuti Chocolates Local artisan chocolates for every SF occasion, from gourmet brunches to beer tastings. (p92)

JEJIM/SHUTTERSTOCK ©

Golden Gate Fortune Cookie Company Make a fortune in San Francisco for 50¢: slip your secret message into a hot cookie here. (p68)

Jade Chocolates Fusion flavor chocolates hit the sweet spot between East and West. (p155)

Vintage

Wasteland Fashion-forward, retro '40s to '80s clothes, plus recent designer scores. (p138)

Loved to Death Creepy Victorian hair lockets and pets taxidermied decades ago. (p138)

Best For Kids

San Francisco has fewer kids per capita than any US city, and according to SF SPCA data, about 20,000 more dogs than children live here. Yet many locals make a living entertaining kids – from Pixar animators to video-game designers – and this town is packed with childish delights.

Junior Foodies

City View Dainty dim sum for discerning young diners. (p64)

Off the Grid Food trucks: the fun way to forage. (p30)

18 Reasons Sign your kid up for classes on pickles and stinky cheeses. (p119)

Humphry Slocombe Freaky ice-cream flavors – including some for the grown-ups. (p119)

Major Thrills

Exploratorium Dare you to try these mad-scientist experiments for yourself... (p51)

Cable cars Look, Mom, no seat belt! (p76)

Musée Mécanique Coin-operated saloon brawls, public executions, Pac-Man and other vintage arcade games. (p37)

Alcatraz Spooky sunset tours of the island prison keep kids on best behavior for weeks. (p49)

Dolores Park Slide down a Mayan pyramid to your picnic table. (p113)

Creative Kids

Children's Creativity Museum Live-action video games and kids' claymation workshops taught by special-effects pros. (p85)

826 Valencia Writing workshops, pirate supplies and fish theater spark active imaginations. (p116)

Flax A dizzying selection of art and craft supplies to fuel your budding *artiste*. (p33)

Kids Gone Wild

California Academy of Sciences Penguins, an eel forest, starfish petting zoos and sleepovers amid rare wildlife. (p144)

Sea lions at Pier 39 Bark back at sea lions lazing around the yacht marina. (p37)

Aquarium of the Bay Walk underwater through glass tubes, as skates flutter past and sharks circle around. (p38)

Best Freebies

Free SF History

Coit Tower Free tours on Wednesday and Saturday mornings cover SF history-redefining murals – including secret stairway gems. (p54)

Balmy Alley Diego Rivera–inspired Mission garage-door murals, from the 1970s to today. (p116)

Beach Chalet Downstairs lobby lined with uplifting Depression-era murals depicting Golden Gate Park history. (p153)

San Francisco Main Library Volunteer-run neighborhood history walking tours (www.sfcityguides.org) and free on-site history exhibits. (p100)

Maritime Museum Ship-shaped 1939 landmark decked out with mosaics and sculpture by African American modernist Sargent Johnson. (p41)

City Hall Free docent-led tours show where the first sit-in happened, and the first gay official was elected...and assassinated. (p100)

Free Art Shows

Clarion Alley The Mission's open-air graffiti gallery constantly unveils new public artworks. (p112)

49 Geary Free contemporary-art shows across four floors, plus free wine on the first Thursday evening of each month. (p85)

Luggage Store Gallery Street artists earn museum cred at this urban art nonprofit. (p100)

SF MOMA The expansion includes 45,000 sq ft of free-to-the-public art spaces. (p80)

Free Entertainment

Amoeba Music Concerts From Elvis Costello to Lana Del Ray, everyone plays free in the back of this music store. (p138)

PATRICK CIVELLO/SHUTTERSTOCK ©

Dolores Park summer movies Family-friendly fare, especially movies set in SF. Expect snark about Mrs Doubtfire's drag. (p113)

Giants Stadium The local crowd at Waterfront Promendade may grant you a spot where you can watch for free, especially if you bring beer. (p90)

Sea lions at Pier 39 Sea-mammal slapstick on yacht marina docks. (p37)

Best Entertainment

Theater & Comedy

American Conservatory Theater Breakthrough premieres and provocative original plays, from Tony Kushner to David Mamet. (p90)

Magic Theatre Cutting-edge theater inside a creatively repurposed waterfront army base. (p32)

Cobb's Comedy Club HBO and NBC talents try their riskiest material here first. (p67)

Beach Blanket Babylon Disney drag satire with giant hats and no mercy – a true San Francisco treat. (p66)

Oberlin Dance Collective Raw and risky performances September to December, and 200 dance classes a week year-round. (p124)

Cinema

Castro Theatre Deco movie palace featuring silver-screen classics and cult hits for cinemaniac audiences. (p129)

Roxie Cinema Film festivals, documentaries and rare cult classics. (p124)

Sports

San Francisco Giants SF's Major League Baseball team is on a World Series winning streak, with beards and women's underwear for luck. (p90)

Golden State Warriors The Bay Area's National Basketball Association team plays basketball to win, and took the championship home to Oakland in 2015 and 2017. Pending completion of

Giant Mitt sculpture, by Scientific Art Studio

a new Warriors stadium, they'll be moving back to San Francisco in 2019.

San Francisco 49ers After they moved 38 miles away to Santa Clara's new Levi's Stadium in 2014, some fans argued the National Football League team should be renamed. To reach the stadium, take Caltrain one hour south to Santa Clara station, then catch the game-day shuttle.

Survival Guide

Survival Guide

Before You Go

When to Go

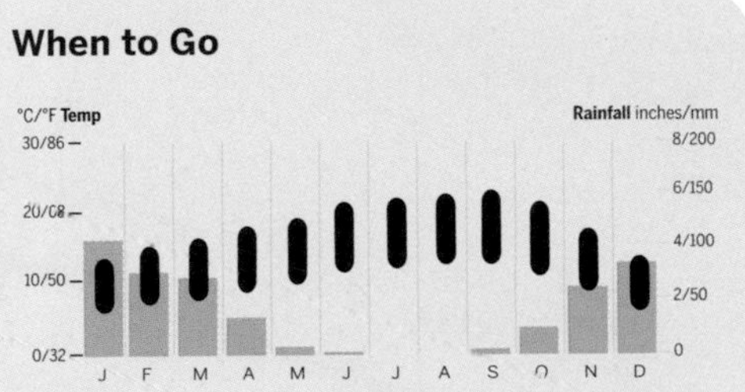

➡ **Winter (Dec–Feb)** Low-season rates, brisk but rarely cold days, and the colorful Lunar New Year parade.

➡ **Spring (Mar–Apr)** Film festivals, blooming parks and midseason rates make the occasional damp day worthwhile.

➡ **Summer (May–Aug)** Street fairs, farmers markets and June Pride celebrations compensate for high-season rates and chilly afternoon fog.

➡ **Fall (Sep–Nov)** Prime time for blue skies, free concerts, better hotel rates and flavor-bursting harvest cuisine.

Book Your Stay

➡ San Francisco's 16.25% hotel tax is not included in most quoted rates.

➡ Downtown hotels offer bargain rates, but avoid the sketchy, depressing Tenderloin district west of Mason St.

➡ Most motels offer free on-site parking. At downtown hotels, expect to pay $35 to $50 for overnight parking.

Useful Websites

➡ **B&B San Francisco** (www.bbsf.com) Personable, privately owned B&Bs and neighborhood inns.

➡ **Hotel Tonight** (www.hoteltonight.com) SF-based hotel-search app offering discount last-minute bookings.

➡ **Lonely Planet** (www.lonelyplanet.com/usa/san-francisco/hotels) Expert author reviews, user feedback, booking engine.

Best Budget

➡ **HI San Francisco Fisherman's Wharf** (415-771-7277; www.sfhostels.com; Fort Mason, Bldg 240; dm $30-53, r $116-134; P @ ; 28, 30, 47, 49) Waterfront hostel with million-dollar views.

➡ **San Remo Hotel** (415-776-8688, 800-352-7366; www.sanremohotel.com; 2237 Mason St; r without bath $119-159; @ ; 30, 47, Powell-Mason) Spartan furnishings, shared bathrooms, great rates.

➡ **Pacific Tradewinds Hostel** (415-433-7970; www.san-francisco-hostel.com; 680 Sacramento St; dm $35-45; front desk 8am-midnight; @ ; 1, California, B Montgomery) Downtown hostel with snappy design.

Best Midrange

➡ **Inn at the Presidio** (415-800-7356; www.innatthepresidio.com; 42 Moraga Ave; r $295-380; P @ ; 43, PresidiGo shuttle) Small luxury inn surrounded by national-park land.

➡ **Kensington Park Hotel** (415-788-6400, 800-553-1900; www.kensingtonparkhotel.com; 450 Post St; r $234-337; @ ; Powell-Hyde, Powell-Mason, M Powell, B Powell) Spiffy Union Sq boutique hotel.

➡ **Hotel Carlton** (415-673-0242, 800-922-7586; www.hotelcarltonsf.com; 1075 Sutter St; r $269-309; @ ; 2, 3, 19, 38, 47, 49) Freshly redesigned with good-value rooms.

➡ **Marker** (415-292-0100, 844-736-2753; http://themarkersanfrancisco.com; 501 Geary St; r from $209; @ ; 38, Powell-Hyde, Powell-Mason) Snazzy design, useful amenities, central location.

➡ **Golden Gate Hotel** (800-835-1118, 415-392-3702; www.goldengatehotel.com; 775 Bush St; r $215, without bath $145; @ ; 2, 3, Powell-Hyde, Powell-Mason) Old-fashioned small hotel with resident cat.

➡ **Coventry Motor Inn** (415-567-1200; www.coventrymotorinn.com; 1901 Lombard St; r $158-228; P ; 22, 28, 30, 43) Value-priced plain-Jane motel with big rooms.

Best Top End

➡ **Hotel Drisco** (415-346-2880, 800-634-7277; www.hoteldrisco.com; 2901 Pacific Ave; r $338-475; @ ; 3, 24) Luxury inn atop Pacific Heights.

➡ **Loews Regency** (844-271-6289, 415-276-9888; www.loewshotels.com/regency-san-francisco; 222 Sansome St; r from $600; @ ; California, M Montgomery, B Montgomery) Five-star service, knockout views.

➡ **Palace Hotel** (415-512-1111; www.sfpalace.com; 2 New Montgomery St; r from $300; @ ; M Montgomery, B Montgomery) Stately classical hotel, century-old landmark.

➡ **Hotel Zetta** (415-543-8555, booking 888-720-7004; www.hotelzetta.com; 55 5th St; r from $324; @ ; B Powell St, M Powell St) Tech-centric downtowner filled with art.

➡ **Argonaut Hotel** (800-790-1415, 415-563-0800; www.argonauthotel.com; 495 Jefferson St; r from $389; P ; 19, 47, 49, Powell-Hyde) Nautical-themed hotel at Fisherman's Wharf.

Arriving in San Francisco

San Francisco Airport (SFO)

➡ **BART** Direct 30-minute ride to/from downtown San Francisco costs $8.95; SFO BART station is outside the international terminal.

➡ **Door-to-door vans** Shared vans depart outside baggage claim; 45 minutes to most SF locations; one-way fares $17 to $20. Companies include **SuperShuttle** (800-258-3826; www.supershuttle.com), **Quake City** (415-255-4899; www.quakecityshuttle.com), **Lorrie's** (415-334-

9000; www.gosfovan.com) and **American Airporter Shuttle** (☎415-202-0733; www.americanairporter.com).

➡ **Express bus** Take **SamTrans** (☎800-660-4287; www.samtrans.com) to Transbay Transit Center ($2.25).

➡ **Taxis** Depart from outside baggage claim; $40 to $55 to most SF destinations.

➡ **Car** Downtown San Francisco is a 20- to 60-minute, 14-mile trip north from SFO up Hwy 101.

Oakland International Airport (OAK)

➡ **BART** BART people-mover shuttles run every 10 to 20 minutes from Terminal 1 to the Coliseum station, where you connect with BART trains to downtown SF ($10.20, 25 minutes).

➡ **Door-to-door vans** Shared rides to SF run $30 to $40 on **Super-Shuttle** (☎800-258-3826; www.supershuttle.com).

➡ **Taxis** Depart curbside; fares $60 to $80 to SF.

San Jose International Airport (SJC)

➡ **Caltrain** The VTA Airport Flyer (bus 10; tickets free, 5am to 11:30pm) departs every 15 to 30 minutes to Santa Clara station, where trains depart to San Francisco. Caltrain terminal is at the corner of 4th and King Sts (one way $9.25, 90 minutes); see www.caltrain.com for details.

➡ **Car** Downtown San Francisco is 50 miles north of SJC, via Hwy 101.

Emeryville Amtrak Station (EMY)

➡ **Train Amtrak** (☎800-872-7245; www.amtrakcalifornia.com) serves San Francisco via Emeryville (near Oakland), and runs free shuttle buses from its Emeryville station to San Francisco's Ferry Building and Caltrain station.

Getting Around

Cable Car

➡ **Best for...** scenic routes and handling hills between downtown and Fisherman's Wharf and North Beach.

➡ **Tickets** Cost $7 per ride (no on/off privileges). Purchase on board from conductor or at cable-car turnaround kiosks.

➡ **Passes** For multiple rides, get a Muni Passport (one/three/seven days $21/32/42).

➡ **Seating** Each car seats about 30, plus standing passengers clinging to straps. To secure a seat, get on at cable-car turnarounds.

Streetcar

➡ **Best for...** travel to the Castro and Ocean Beach and along Market St and the Embarcadero to Fisherman's Wharf.

➡ **Muni streetcar** The N Judah line connects SoMa, downtown and Ocean Beach. The F line connects Fisherman's Wharf to the Castro via the Embarcadero and Market St. The Muni Street & Transit Map is available free online (www.sfmta.com).

➡ **Tickets** Standard fares cost $2.50 (exact change required).

➡ **Schedules** Around 5am to midnight weekdays; limited schedules on weekends. For route-planning and schedules, consult http://transit.511.org; for real-time departures, see www.nextmuni.com.

➡ **Night service** L and N lines operate 24 hours, but above-ground 'Owl' buses replace streetcars between 12:30am and 5:30am.

Key Routes & Destinations

➡ **F** Fisherman's Wharf & Embarcadero to Castro.

➡ **J** Downtown to Mission/Castro.

➡ **K, L, M** Downtown to Castro.

➡ **N** Caltrain and AT&T Park to Haight, Golden Gate Park and Ocean Beach.

➡ **T** Embarcadero to Caltrain and Bayview.

BART

➡ **Best for...** travel between downtown and the Mission, East Bay and SFO.

➡ **Destinations** Downtown, Mission District, SF and Oakland international airports, Berkeley and Oakland.

➡ **Tickets** Sold in BART station machines; fares start at $1.95.

➡ **Schedules** Consult http://transit.511.org.

Bus

➡ **Best for...** travel to/from the Haight, Marina and the Avenues.

➡ **Muni** SF's bus, streetcar and cable car lines are operated by Muni.

➡ **Tickets** Standard fare $2.50; buy on board (exact change required) and at underground Muni stations. Keep ticket for transfers (good for 90 minutes on streetcars and buses), and to avoid a $100 fine.

➡ **Schedules** On digital bus-stop displays and maps, plus http://transit.511.org; for real-time departures, see www.nextmuni.com. Weekend and evening service is limited.

➡ **Night service** 'Owl' service (1am to 5am) offered on limited lines, with departures every 30 to 60 minutes; Late Night Transfers valid for travel 8:30pm to 5:30am.

➡ **System map** Available free online (www.sfmta.com).

Taxi

➡ Best for... SoMa and Mission club nights.

➡ **Fares** Meters start at $3.50 plus about $2.75 per mile and 10% tip ($1 minimum).

➡ **Taxi services** Companies with 24-hour dispatches include **DeSoto Cab** (☎415-970-1300; http://flywheeltaxi.com/), **Luxor** (☎415-282-4141; www.luxorcab.com) and **Yellow Cab** (☎415-333-3333; www.yellowcabsf.com).

Bicycle

➡ **Best for...** sightseeing along the waterfront and west of Van Ness Ave.

➡ **Rentals** Near Golden Gate Park and Fisherman's Wharf.

Car

➡ **Best for...** trips out of town. Avoid driving in

Transit Passes

➡ **Muni Passport** Allows unlimited travel on all Muni transport, including cable cars; it's sold at the Muni kiosk at the Powell St cable car turnaround on Market St, San Francisco Visitor Information Center, the TIX Bay Area kiosk at Union Square and shops around town – see www.sfmta.com for exact locations. One-day passports can be purchased from cable-car conductors.

➡ **Clipper Cards** Downtown Muni/BART stations issue the Clipper Card: a reloadable transit card with a $3 minimum valid for Muni, BART, Caltrain and Golden Gate Transit (not cable cars). Clipper cards automatically deduct fares and apply transfers; only one Muni fare is deducted in a 90-minute period.

San Francisco; traffic is constant, street parking scarce, hills tricky and meter-readers ruthless.

➡ **Garages** Around $2 to $8 per hour ($25 to $50 per day) downtown. For public parking garages, see www.sfmta.com; for a map of garages and rates, see http://sfpark.org. Ask hotels, restaurants and entertainment venues about validation.

➡ **Rentals** Start at $55 per day, $175 to $300 per week, plus 8.75% sales tax and insurance.

➡ **Car share** Prius Hybrids and Minis are rented by the hour with **Zipcar** (☎866-494-7227; www.zipcar.com) for flat rates (including gas and insurance) starting at $8.25 per hour ($89 per day); $25 application fee and $50 prepaid usage required in advance.

➡ **Rush hour** Avoid peak traffic weekdays (7:30am to 9:30am and 4:30pm to 6:30pm); call ☎511 for traffic updates.

➡ **Towed cars** Retrieve cars towed for parking violations at **Autoreturn** (☎415-865-8200; www.autoreturn.com; 450 7th St, SoMa; ⏰24hr; M 27, 42); fines run $73 plus towing and storage fee, starting at $208 for the first four hours.

➡ **Roadside assistance** Members of the **American Automobile Association** (AAA; ☎415-773-1900, 800-222-4357; www.aaa.com; 160 Sutter St; ⏰8:30am-5:30pm Mon-Fri; B Montgomery, M Montgomery) can call the ☎800 number anytime for emergency road service and towing.

Parking Restrictions

➡ **Red** No parking/stopping.

➡ **Blue** Disabled only.

➡ **Green** Ten minutes 9am–6pm.

➡ **White** Pickup/drop-off only.

➡ **Yellow** Loading zone 7am–6pm.

Green Tortoise

Green Tortoise (☎415-956-7500, 800-867-8647; www.greentortoise.com) offers quasi-organized, slow travel on biodiesel-fueled buses with built-in berths from San Francisco to West Coast destinations including Santa Cruz, Death Valley, Big Sur and LA.

Essential Information

Business Hours

Nonstandard hours are listed in reviews; standard business hours are as follows:

Banks 9am to 4:30pm or 5pm Monday to Friday (occasionally 9am to noon Saturday).

Offices 8:30am to 5:30pm Monday to Friday.

Restaurants Breakfast 8am to 10am; lunch 11:30am to 2:30pm; dinner 5:30pm, with last service 9pm to 9:30pm weekdays or 10pm weekends; Saturday and Sunday brunch 10am to 2pm.

Shops 10am to 6pm or 7pm Monday to Saturday, though hours often run 11am to 8pm Saturday, and 11am to 6pm Sunday.

Discount Cards

City Pass (www.citypass.com; adult/child $89/69) Covers cable cars, Muni and entry to four attractions, including the California Academy of Sciences, Blue & Gold Fleet Bay Cruise, the Aquarium of the Bay and either the Exploratorium or the de Young Museum.

Go Card (www.smartdestinations.com; adult/child 1 day $65/49, 2 days $90/62, 3 days $115/85) Provides access to the city's major attractions, including the California Academy of Sciences, the de Young Museum, the Aquarium of the Bay, the Conservatory of Flowers,

the Beat Museum and Go Car tours, plus discounts on packaged tours and waterfront restaurants and cafes.

Electricity

120V/60Hz

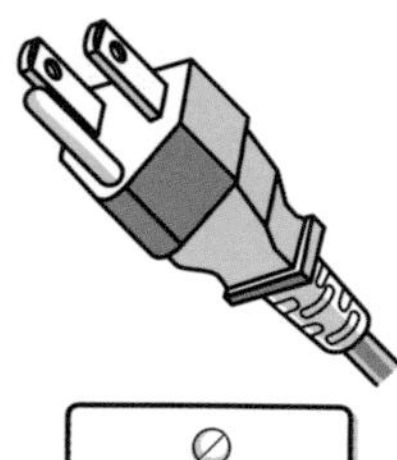

120V/60Hz

Emergencies

- **Police, fire & ambulance** emergencies 911, nonemergencies 311
- **San Francisco General Hospital** (Zuckerberg San Franciso General Hospital and Trauma Center; emergency 415-206-8111, main hospital 415-206-8000; www.sfdph.org; 1001 Potrero Ave; 24hr; 9, 10, 33, 48)
- **Drug & Alcohol Emergency Info Line** (415-362-3400; www.sfsuicide.org)
- **Trauma Recovery & Rape Treatment Center** (24hr hotline 415-206-8125, business hours 415-437-3000; www.traumarecoverycenter.org)

Money

- Most banks have ATMs open 24 hours; service charges may apply.
- The US dollar is the only currency accepted in San Francisco; debit/credit cards are accepted widely.

Changing Money

- **Exchange bureaus** Located at airports, but most city banks offer better rates – try centrally located **Bank of America** (415-837-1394; www.bankamerica.com; 1 Powell St, downstairs; 9am-5pm Mon-Thu, to 6pm Fri, 10am-2pm Sat; M Powell, B Powell).
- **Exchange rates** Consult www.xe.com, a currency converter site.

Credit Cards & Travelers Checks

Some places will accept travelers checks like cash.

To report lost or stolen credit cards or travelers checks, contact the following numbers:

- American Express 415-536-2600
- Diners Club 800-234-6377
- Discover 800-347-2683
- MasterCard 800-622-7747
- Thomas Cook 800-223-7373
- Visa 800-227-6811

Public Holidays

Holidays that may affect business hours and transit schedules include the following:

New Year's Day January 1

Martin Luther King Jr Day Third Monday in January

Presidents' Day Third Monday in February

Easter Sunday (and Good Friday and Easter Monday) March or April

Memorial Day Last Monday in May

Independence Day July 4

Labor Day First Monday in September

Columbus Day Second Monday in October

Veterans Day November 11

Thanksgiving Fourth Thursday in November

Christmas Day December 25

Safe Travel

➡ Keep your city smarts and wits about you, especially in the Tenderloin, SoMa and the Mission.

➡ After dark, Dolores Park, Buena Vista Park and the entry to Golden Gate Park at Haight and Stanyan Sts can turn seedy with petty drug dealing.

➡ Panhandlers and homeless people are part of San Francisco's urban landscape. People will probably ask you for spare change, but donations to local nonprofits stretch further. For safety, don't engage with panhandlers at night or around ATMs. Otherwise, a simple 'I'm sorry' is a polite response.

Telephone

US country code ☎1

San Francisco area code ☎415

International calls From the Bay Area, call ☎011 + country code + area code + number; when calling Canada, skip the ☎011.

Calling other area codes The area code must be preceded by a 1.

Area Codes in the Bay

East Bay ☎510

Marin County ☎415

Peninsula ☎650

San Francisco ☎415

San Jose ☎408

Santa Cruz ☎831

Wine Country ☎707

Operator Services

International ☎00

Local directory ☎411

Long-distance directory information ☎1 + area code + 555-1212

Operator ☎0

Toll-free number information ☎800-555-1212

Toilets

Citywide Self-cleaning, coin-operated outdoor kiosk commodes cost 25¢; there are 25 citywide, mostly in North Beach, Fisherman's Wharf, the Financial District and the Tenderloin. Toilet paper isn't always available, and there's a 20-minute time limit. Public library branches and some city parks also have restrooms.

Downtown Most hotel lobbies have restrooms. Clean toilets and baby-changing tables can be found at **Westfield San Francisco Centre** (www.westfield.com/sanfrancisco; 865 Market St; ⏰10am-8:30pm Mon-Sat, 11am-7pm Sun; 🚻; 🚋Powell-Mason, Powell-Hyde, Ⓜ Powell, Ⓑ Powell) and **Macy's** (www.macys.com; 170 O'Farrell St; ⏰10am-9pm Mon-Sat, 11am-8pm Sun; 🚋Powell-Mason, Powell-Hyde, Ⓜ Powell, Ⓑ Powell).

Civic Center San Francisco Main Library (☎415-557-4400; www.sfpl.org; 100 Larkin St; ⏰10am-6pm Mon & Sat, 9am-8pm Tue-Thu, noon-6pm Fri, noon-5pm Sun; 📶; Ⓜ Civic Center) has restrooms.

Haight-Ashbury & Mission District Woefully lacking in public toilets; you may have to buy a

Money-Saving Tips

➡ Summer festivals in Golden Gate Park and neighborhood street fairs are often free.

➡ One day each month is usually free at SF museums, and some evening events offer steeply discounted admission; see individual listings.

➡ Hang on to your Muni ticket for discounted admission at key attractions, including California Academy of Sciences, de Young Museum and Legion of Honor.

n

n

2000;
sitor-in-
wer level,
Market &
m-5pm Mon-
Sat & Sun (closed
Apr); Powell-
Powell-Hyde, M Pow-
B Powell) Maps, Muni
assports and help with
accommodations.

Golden Gate National Recreation Area Headquarters (GGNRA; ☎415-561-4700; www.nps.gov/goga; 495 Jefferson St; ⏰8:30am-4:30pm Mon-Fri; 🚌E, F, 🚋Powell-Hyde, 🚌19, 30, 47) Find everything hikers need to know about the GGNRA, plus maps and information on camping, hiking and programs at these and other national parks in the Pacific West region (including Yosemite).

Travellers with Disabilities

All Bay Area transit companies offer wheelchair-accessible service and travel discounts for travellers with disabilities. Major car-rental companies can usually supply hand-controlled vehicles with one or two days' notice. For people with visual impairment, major intersections emit a chirping signal to indicate when it is safe to cross the street. Resources:

San Francisco Bay Area Regional Transit Guide (https://511.org/transit/accessibility/overview) Covers accessibility for people with disabilities.

Muni's Street & Transit (www.sfmta.com/getting-around/accessibility) For wheelchair-friendly bus routes and streetcar stops.

Independent Living Resource Center of San Francisco (☎415-543-6222; www.ilrcsf.org; ⏰9am-4:30pm Mon-Thu, to 4pm Fri) Provides further information about wheelchair accessibility on Bay Area public transit and in hotels and other local facilities.

Environmental Traveling Companions (☎415-474-7662; www.etctrips.org) Leads excellent outdoor trips – whitewater rafting, kayaking and cross-country skiing – for kids with disabilities.

Visas

Check the US Department of State (http://travel.state.gov/content/visas/english/visit/visa-waiver-program.html) for updates and details on the following requirements.

- **Canadians** Proof of identity and citizenship required.
- **Visa Waiver Program** The VWP allows nationals from 38 countries to enter the US without a visa. It requires a machine-readable passport issued after November 2006.
- **Visa required** For anyone staying longer than 90 days, or with plans to work or study in the US.

Dos & Don'ts

Fashion Casual is the norm, but pretty much anything goes fashion-wise in San Francisco, from bird costumes to glitter thongs. But there is one rule: don't stare.

Food Vegans, pescatarians and allergies are accommodated at many restaurants – but confirm when you call for reservations so the chef can adjust recipes and use separate utensils as needed. Don't be shy about asking about food sourcing – many SF restaurants are proud to serve local, organic, humane, sustainable fare.

Politics Leftist politics are mainstream in San Francisco, as is friendly debate. Don't be shy about sharing your views, and do hear out others.

Behind the Scenes

Send Us Your Feedback

We love to hear from travelers – your comments help make our books be read every word, and we guarantee that your feedback goes straight to the Visit **lonelyplanet.com/contact** to submit your updates and suggestions.

Note: We may edit, reproduce and incorporate your comments in Lonely Pla products such as guidebooks, websites and digital products, so let us know if you don't want your comments reproduced or your name acknowledged. For a copy of our privacy policy visit lonelyplanet.com/privacy.

Alison's Thanks

Thanks to Cliff Wilkinson, Sarah Sung, Lisa Park, DeeAnn Budney, PT Tenenbaum, and above all, Marco Flavio Marinucci, for making a Muni bus ride into the adventure of a lifetime.

John's Thanks

Thanks to destination editor Clifton Wilkinson and my co-author Alison Bing, with whom it's always lovely to work. And most of all, thanks to you, dear reader – you make my life so joyful and I'm grateful for the honor of being your guide through the cool grey city of love.

Acknowledgements

Cover photograph: Lombard St, Russian Hill, San Francisco; Susanne Kremer/4Corners ©

This Book

This 6th edition of Lonely Planet's *Pocket San Francisco* guidebook was curated by Mariella Krause, and researched and written by Alison Bing and John A Vlahides. The previous edition was also written by Alison Bing and John A Vlahides. This guidebook was produced by the following:

Destination Editors Clifton Wilkinson, Sarah Stocking

Product Editors Will Allen, Ronan Abayawickrema

Regional Senior Cartographer Alison Lyall

Cartographer Julie Dodkins

Book Designer Jessica Rose

Assisting Editors Sarah Bailey, Andrew Bain, Judith Bamber, Andrea Dobbin, Carly Hall, Victoria Harrison, Kellie Langdon, Jodie Martire, Charlotte Orr

Cover Researcher Marika Mercer

Thanks to Michelle Coxall, Sasha Drew, Lis Ellis, Sara Garcia, Shona Gray, Kate James, Katherine Marsh, Anne Mason, Jenna Myers, Kathryn Rowan, Vicky Smith, Tony Wheeler

x

See also separate subindexes for:

- Eating p189
- Drinking p190
- Entertainment p191
- Shopping p191

Sights 000
Map Pages **000**

Sights 000
Map Pages **000**

Eating

Drinking

Entertainment

Sights 000
Map Pages **000**

Shopping

Our Writers

Mariella Krause

Mariella Krause loves nothing more than to see travelers on the streets of San Francisco clutching a Lonely Planet guide that she contributed to. Don't be surprised if she stops and asks you if you need directions. This is her twentieth title for Lonely Planet.

Alison Bing

Over 10 guidebooks and 20 years in San Francisco, author Alison Bing has spent more time on Alcatraz than some inmates, become an aficionado of drag and burritos, and willfully ignored Muni signs warning that safety requires avoiding unnecessary conversation.

John A Vlahides

John A Vlahides has been a cook in a Parisian bordello, a luxury-hotel concierge, a television host, a safety monitor in a sex club and a French–English interpreter, and he is one of Lonely Planet's most experienced and prolific guidebook authors.

Published by Lonely Planet Global Limited
CRN 554153
6th edition – December 2017
ISBN 978 1 78657 355 1

10 9 8 7 6 5 4 3 2 1
Printed in Singapore